"What a wonderful, motivating treatment of the much-neglected and yet extremely important subject of biblical encouragement! Not only will you be helped by reading this but others will be helped because you did."

—Jeffery Smith, pastor of Emmanuel
Baptist Church, Coconut Creek, Florida

"Our Lord and His apostles were at pains to motivate their friends by great positive encouragement, and it is this rich seam that Mark Chanski mines in this important book. One prominent feature of vibrant contemporary congregations is that they are fellowships of encouragement, and one means of attaining this blessing will be the thoughtful study of this book."

—Geoff Thomas, pastor for fifty years of Alfred Place
Baptist Church, Aberystwyth, Wales

"This exhilarating, gospel-centered book is a must-read for the body of Christ that at times, sadly, has been labeled as a group that 'shoots its own wounded.' This Scripture-saturated, grace-filled volume is a wonderful corrective for the church and with the blessing of God can be a powerful catalyst to positively transform local assemblies into places where healthy biblical encouragement is more the rule than the exception. I highly recommend it."

—Rob Ventura, pastor of Grace Community
Baptist Church, North Providence, Rhode Island

"Encouragement is a gracious gift to be recognized, developed, and— I have no doubt—encouraged. It might sound slightly different in different cultures and places, but it is a holy skill worth learning and using. Surveying principles and practices, Mark Chanski provides us with earnest and thoughtful encouragements to become encouragers. If you are starved of encouragement yourself or if you have starved others of it, then this book will point you in a healthier, holier, and happier direction."

—Jeremy Walker, pastor of Maidenbower
Baptist Church, Crawley, United Kingdom

ENCOURAGEMENT

ENCOURAGEMENT
Adrenaline for the Soul

Mark Chanski

Reformation Heritage Books
Grand Rapids, Michigan

Reformation Heritage Books
2965 Leonard St. NE
Grand Rapids, MI 49525
616–977–0889
orders@heritagebooks.org
www.heritagebooks.org

Printed in the United States of America
19 20 21 22 23 24/10 9 8 7 6 5 4 3 2 1

Library of Congress Cataloging-in-Publication Data

Names: Chanski, Mark, author.
Title: Encouragement : adrenaline for the soul / Mark Chanski.
Description: Grand Rapids, Michigan : Reformation Heritage Books, 2019. | Includes bibliographical references and index.
Identifiers: LCCN 2019016241 (print) | LCCN 2019019986 (ebook) | ISBN 9781601786630 (epub) | ISBN 9781601786623 (pbk. : alk. paper)
Subjects: LCSH: Encouragement—Religious aspects—Christianity.
Classification: LCC BV4647.E53 (ebook) | LCC BV4647.E53 C43 2019 (print) | DDC 248.4—dc23
LC record available at https://lccn.loc.gov/2019016241

For additional Reformed literature, request a free book list from Reformation Heritage Books at the above regular or email address.

To my departed brother Ted Christman, that St. Bernard of a man who, like a big, thick, furry-coated dog wearing a collar with a barrel flask full of restoring medicinal swallows, bounded through the snowdrifts toward us with timely expressions of encouragement when our fainting souls needed it most.

CONTENTS

PREFACE

This book is filled with quotations, historical references, illustrations, and examples related to the virtue of giving encouragement. Such allusions are not blanket endorsements of anyone's entire life or body of work. Winston Churchill, for example, is cited as a noble model of encouragement for the United Kingdom in its darkest hour. But this does not deny that Prime Minister Churchill was a historical figure riddled with flaws in both lifestyle and creed. Nobility and wisdom can and should be recognized even in defective people.

The writer to the Hebrews in chapter 11, his spiritual hall of fame, praises virtue and nobility in such dubious characters as Barak, Samson, and Jephthah, even though they did things that make us wince and blush (v. 32). Even the more high-profile patriarchs referenced there, like Noah (v. 7), Abraham (v. 8), Jacob (v. 21), and David (v. 32), who are lifted up as our spiritual models, have stories checkered with foolish, shameful, and questionable exploits. Did I mention Rahab the harlot (v. 31)?

On Mars Hill Paul used inspiring quotations from two insightful Greek poets—Epimenides the Cretan and Aratus the Cilician.[1] But neither of them were orthodox and safe guides theologically or philosophically. In teaching His disciples about the virtue of discerning foresight, even our Lord Jesus references the example of an

---

1. F. F. Bruce, *The Book of the Acts*, rev. ed., The New International Commentary on the New Testament (Grand Rapids: Eerdmans, 2008), 359–60.

unrighteous steward (Luke 16:1–13). When urging them to persistence in prayer, He cites the behavior of an unjust judge (18:1–8).

In keeping with this teaching style, the Puritans unapologetically made ample references to noble traits in questionable characters such as Alexander the Great, Aristotle, and Julius Caesar. The Puritans heartily recognized these figures' sparks of greatness without endorsing their entire careers.

It is in this healthy tradition that I have made ample use of fallen humanity. We are all broken toys on this "Island of Misfits," and none of us can be lifted up as unqualified paragons of excellence. There is only One who is good and needs no qualification (Mark 10:18).

ACKNOWLEDGMENTS

The Lord has been so gracious to give me many wise counselors and helpers who have directly assisted me in the writing and publishing of this book. I can mention only a few.

Rob Ventura, who early on told me that the encouragement theme was crucial and helped push open some doors; Kevin Filcik, my fellow pastor, who has been a more encouraging friend to me than Samwise Gamgee to Mr. Frodo; Dr. Joel Beeke, who gave a green light to edit and publish a manuscript that still needed work; David Woollin, whose savvy advice and counsel have been priceless to me; Jay Collier, who kindly worked through a number of viewpoint differences with grace and tenderness; Annette Gysen, who loved me as a gifted editor by giving me the faithful blows of a friend, making the book much better; Gary Hendrix, my highly esteemed brother and mentor, who read through an early version, told me it was a bull's-eye theme, yet gave me better aim on an important area; Jared Chanski, our firstborn son, who untied a Gordian knot in reorganizing some chapter snags that had left me with writer's block; Calvin Chanski, our second-born son, who persuaded me to rewrite the crucial opening chapter according to his new and improved blueprint; Austin Chanski, our third-born son, whose three children have qualified me to write with experience on grandparenting; Nathan Chanski, our fourth-born son, who designed the cover that made me laugh with "Eureka" delight when I first saw it; Abigail Chanski, our only daughter, whose encouraging personality epitomizes what this book is all about; and Dianne, my intelligent, beautiful, and servant-hearted Abigail, who does good to me all the days of her life, and frequently endured my writer's preoccupied thoughts and blank stares out the windows.

INTRODUCTION

Let there be something of benevolence, in all that I speak.

—Jonathan Edwards, 70th and final
Resolution, August 17, 1723

Why write a book on encouragement? Why not write about something important—like the gospel? Encouragement? Sounds like something right out of our politically correct, pampering culture, or something an ego-stroking motivational speaker would address.

I understand that reaction. So does pastor, author, and seminary professor David Murray. Regarding some gospel-loving Christians' reluctance to give encouragement, he writes, "Sometimes even Reformed Theology, or I should say an imbalanced Reformed Theology could deter expressions of appreciation. 'Affirming good works? Don't we believe in total depravity?' 'Praising people will only make them proud; isn't humbling people our aim?' 'Soli Deo Gloria! Where does people-praise enter the picture?'"[1]

Let me explain why this book is important. The gospel gloriously reveals the one thing needful—the good news that we, as hell-deserving sinners, can get right with God through the redemptive work of His Son, Jesus Christ. That magnificent truth satisfies our vertical and eternal needs by reconciling us to our

---

1. David Murray, "Practicing Affirmation," *Ligonier Blog*, Ligonier Ministries, https://www.ligonier.org/blog/practicing-affirmation/.

Maker, who becomes our eternal Abba Father. What could be more encouraging?

So the questions come: Who, then, needs any more encouraging? Shouldn't that be enough? And if we put an emphasis on human encouragement, aren't we robbing God of His due and directing eyes away from Him to people? Why descend from the sublimely vertical and divine to the mundanely horizontal and human?

We do well here to remember the two great commandments: love the Lord with all your strength, and love your neighbor as yourself (see Mark 12:30–31). We are solemnly obligated to love God vertically and, by virtue of the saving work of Christ in our soul by His Spirit, to love one another horizontally. Loving God and loving one another aren't mutually exclusive, but inseparably intertwined. God's formula for personal flourishing prescribes a combination of both divine (vertical) and human (horizontal) love.

I was recently strolling a country road in my rural neighborhood. I passed by the home of an elderly Christian woman, Alma, the widow of my farmer friend Roger, who died a few years ago. Roger left Alma alone to care for their son Dale, who struggles with the debilitating effects of a long-ago automobile accident. I spied some rubbish beyond the shoulder of the road in the tall grass lawn on Alma's property. It was the electrical motor of a garage door opener. Somebody's jagged trash had ended up in Alma's tall grass, and I feared that when Alma next mowed her lawn she would blindly drive over it and tear up the blades on her lawn tractor. What a nightmare for a poor widow!

My self-centered instinct was just to walk by. But eventually I saw things clearly. If Alma was to flourish, she needed love. I suppose I could have left a gospel tract in her mailbox and reminded her of God's divine love in Christ's sacrifice. But the gospel was calling me to step into her life and practically extend to her my human love by taking action. So I picked up that filthy motor, weighing about twenty-five pounds, and carried it about a quarter mile to my garage, where I tossed it into my trash dumpster.

It reminded me of Boaz during the times of the Judges, who saw the poor widow Ruth hungrily gleaning in his fields. He gave her a gospel-tract blessing by shouting out, "The LORD repay your work, and a full reward be given you by the LORD God of Israel, under whose *wings* [Hebrew *canaf*] you have come for refuge" (Ruth 2:12). The modern Christianity version of this would be reciting Philippians 4:19: "And my God shall supply all your need according to His riches in glory by Christ Jesus." But it could be that Boaz's blessing sounded a bit hollow in the ears of the Lord, like, "Depart in peace, be warmed and filled" (James 2:16).

By the story's end, we find that God intended for Boaz to incarnate the Lord's vertical divine love by practically extending his own human horizontal love. God's call for Boaz to personally provide Ruth's needs came on the threshing floor when Ruth proposed to Boaz: "I am Ruth, your maidservant. Take your maidservant under your *wing* [Hebrew *canaf*], for you are a close relative" (Ruth 3:9). Boaz then married Ruth, caring for her every practical need. The wordplay language profoundly teaches that the Lord's wings are typically incarnated into people's helpings. God vertically supplies needs by horizontally enlisting hands.

The jagged motor was hidden in the tall grass. The widow Alma needed love. God provided by enlisting my hands.

Daily, we stroll past our neighbors—both believers and unbelievers. They are needy, just like we are. Their yards are cluttered with the rubble of a sin-cursed world, leaving them discouraged on many levels. Our great commission is to love our neighbors as ourselves by conveying to them the gospel-inspired, Spirit-infused love of God on many levels.

When a Christian couple met two parentless boys in the dirty rubble of a Romanian orphanage, they didn't just evangelize them— they adopted them. They didn't just direct them to the heavenly Father, but gave themselves as an earthly father and mother the boys could touch and feel and hear. Filling a believing or unbelieving boy's love tank with parental love harmonizes beautifully with the gospel and the boy's ultimate need for divine love. When we find someone in the rubble of discouraging circumstances, gospel love doesn't call us merely to evangelize them, only directing them to their heavenly Father; we should encourage that person, filling his or her soul with kindhearted brotherly love. Just as human parenting is loving, so also human encouraging is loving.

This is why we have entire books focused on such issues as adopting, parenting, pastoring, befriending, and encouraging from a biblical perspective. The Bible is teeming with revelation that calls us to love one another by mutual encouragement. That is what this book is about.

Our politically correct culture has perversely twisted and contorted this theme of encouragement. Ego-stroking false teachers of the prosperity gospel have heretically and idolatrously abused it. But that is all the more reason for us to biblically reevaluate and examine it. Simply because something is abusable doesn't mean it is disposable. Grace can be abused, as can church and parental discipline. But we dispose of them to our peril. The same is true of encouragement.

David Murray helps us again: "In light of these substantial personal, societal, and theological obstacles [to encouragement], we need lots of biblical warrant to help us climb up, over, and into a more positive, affirming, and encouraging life. And being novices at this, we also need lots of hand-holding and step-by-step guidance on how to do this in a helpful and God-honoring way."[2] That is what I seek to accomplish with this book.

While finishing up the last chapter of this book, I received an out-of-the-blue message from a young man in his late twenties who has been sent out by his local congregation to plant a church in a distant state. He wrote to thank me for a sermon I preached in his home church a dozen years earlier on the theme of encouragement. He said, "I'm not exaggerating to say that that sermon in many ways set the trajectory for me for how I wanted to use my speech to uplift others. From that day forward I purposed to be

---

2. Murray, "Practicing Affirmation."

the sort of Christian who regularly endeavors to encourage others. I have frequently gone back to that sermon in my mind to fuel my efforts at encouraging my brothers and sisters in the body of Christ."

That is precisely the impact I aim for with this book, which interestingly grew out of that dozen-year-old sermon. I seek not only to instruct and educate with biblical truth but also to inspire and motivate with compelling conviction. I want the rank-and-file reader to put the book down, constrained in soul to be a man or woman on a mission and make this resolution: "So help me God, I will from this day forward be an encourager."

May the Lord use this book for our good and His glory!

The Exhilaration of
ENCOURAGEMENT

Death and life are in the power of the tongue.
—Proverbs 18:21

On January 23, 1936, Myrtle Kramer gave birth to her little boy Jerry in Jordan, Montana. But Jerry Kramer didn't stay little for long. Myrtle's darling eventually grew to be six feet three inches, weighed 245 pounds, and played football for the University of Idaho. In 1958 he was drafted into the professional ranks by the Green Bay Packers as an offensive lineman, a guard. During Jerry's first-year rookie season, Green Bay was the laughingstock of the league, with a record of one win, ten losses, and one tie—not the kind of success either Jerry or Myrtle would have hoped for. And things got worse for him the following year. In 1959, embarrassed by their nightmare season, the Packers hired a new head coach, the former offensive coach of the New York Giants, Vince Lombardi.

When the preseason summer workouts began, Kramer, the big, insecure Montana country boy, wondered how he would fare under the new regime. Uptight and plagued with self-doubt, he made a poor first impression during the early practice field workouts. It all came to a head during a goal-line scrimmage, when Kramer couldn't seem to do anything right. He was jumping offside, missing his assignments, getting late to his blocks, and all the while the new coaching staff was yelling criticisms at him. Disoriented and suffocating in failure, he was on the verge of quitting football altogether right then and there. Defeated, Kramer crawled back to the locker room. There he sat on a bench in front of his locker with his elbows on his knees and his face in his hands, trying to decide whether to quit that day or wait until the end of the season.

In walked Lombardi, and he did something that would have made Myrtle's heart sing. This future legend and Hall of Fame coach, after whom the Super Bowl trophy is now named, sized up the locker-room drama, walked over, messed up Kramer's sweaty hair, and said, "Son, someday you're going to be one of the greatest guards in football." Then Lombardi walked out. That was it. But something happened. That word of encouragement transformed Jerry Kramer. The timid weakling became a heroic Hercules.

That timely word of locker-room encouragement from Lombardi was a defining moment. Kramer claims that from that day forward he was a changed man. Lombardi's encouraging comment at a discouraging moment shot Kramer, athletically speaking, to football greatness. He got up from that bench and never turned back. He became a Green Bay starter and ended up anchoring the Packer's offensive line for years, dominating defensive foes with Hercules-like strength. He is best known for throwing what is called the most famous block in NFL history, manhandling six feet six Jethro Pugh of the Dallas Cowboys, which paved the way for quarterback Bart Starr to score the winning touchdown to seal the 1967 world championship game. Kramer led his team to a pro football dynasty of five league championships. Five times Kramer was voted to the all-star team as an All-Pro offensive guard, and in 2018 he joined Coach Lombardi when he was inducted into the Hall of Fame.[1]

---

1. Mike Voight, *The Sports Leadership Playbook: Principles and Techniques for Coaches and Captains* (Jefferson, N.C.: McFarland, 2014), 125.

Kramer condensed it well: "There was something about Lombardi that brought out the best that a man could give."[2] A big part of that something was Lombardi's timely words of encouragement.

Encouragement Is Like Adrenaline

It is a vivid picture—a timid weakling transformed into a heroic Hercules. Isn't that just the stuff of ancient myths and modern fictional superheroes? No, it really happens. People can chemically and physiologically undergo superhero-like transformations. And adrenaline can do it.

In 2012, Lauren Kornacki, a twenty-two-year-old woman in Glen Allen, Virginia, lifted a portion of a BMW 525i off her father when the car toppled from a jack.[3] In 2006, Tom Boyle, a man in Tucson, Arizona, hoisted part of a Chevy Camaro off a trapped, screaming, and bleeding bicyclist.[4] Lifting enormous things can be Hercules-like, and so can fighting fierce foes. In 2006, Lydia Angyiou went toe-to-toe with a polar bear in northern Quebec. She ran toward and tackled the beast to protect her son and his friends while they played hockey.[5] Chemically and physiologically speaking, what happened in these three cases to transform the weaklings into Hercules? Adrenaline happened.

A chief factor in pushing the body to extremes is the well-known "adrenaline rush," in which hormones such as epinephrine (also known as adrenaline) surge out of our adrenal glands, into our blood, and throughout the body. Gordon Lynch, a physiologist

---

2. Jerry Kramer, interview by Dennis Prager, *Dennis Prager Show*, February 2011.

3. Alyssa Newcomb, "Super Strength: Daughter Rescues Dad Pinned Under Car," *ABC News*, August 1, 2012, https://abcnews.go.com/US/superhero-woman -lifts-car-off-dad/story?id=16907591.

4. Alexis Huicochea, "Man Lifts Car Off Pinned Cyclist," Tucson.com, July 28, 2006, http://tucson.com/news/local/crime/article_e7f04bbd-309b-5c7e-808d -1907d91517ac.html.

5. Paul Waldie, "Protective Mother Wrestles Lost Polar Bear," *The Globe and Mail*, February 21, 2006, https://www.theglobeandmail.com/news/national /protective-mother-wrestles-lost-polar-bear/article703773/.

at the University of Melbourne, Australia, explains, "The release of adrenaline is rapid—seemingly instantaneous—so that we can respond accordingly to fight-or-flight situations."[6]

Adrenaline dramatically boosts breathing and heart rate, flooding our muscles with extra, oxygenated blood for more forceful exertions. Nerves from the spinal cord running to our bodies' muscles are more easily able to recruit motor units, again harnessing more of a muscle's potential strength. "The more motor units that are recruited, the greater the force that can be developed," says Lynch.[7] The product is what physiologists call "hysterical strength"—the exertion of extreme power and energy by humans beyond what is believed to be normal.

The internal physiological drama is fascinating. When alarmed by a sudden emergency crisis, the human body transforms. The stressor—for example, the sight of a loved one pinned beneath a car or charged by a bear—stimulates the hypothalamus. This region of the brain maintains the balance between stress and relaxation in the body. When alerted to danger, it sends out a chemical signal to the adrenal glands, activating the sympathetic system, sending the body into an excited state. These glands release adrenaline (epinephrine), a hormone that creates the state of readiness helping a human confront danger. Adrenaline raises heart rate, increases respiration, dilates the pupils, slows down digestion, and—perhaps most importantly—allows muscles to contract extraordinarily.[8]

Bursts of adrenaline during stressful situations can boost abilities far beyond the muscular. Senses of vision, hearing, and touch are dramatically heightened. Thinking clarifies and is energized. Frames of mind change from timidity, insecurity, and self-doubt

---

6. Adam Hadhazy, "How It's Possible for an Ordinary Person to Lift a Car," May 2, 2016, "BBC Future," *BBC*, http://www.bbc.com/future/story/20160501 -how-its-possible-for-an-ordinary-person-to-lift-a-car.

7. Hadhazy, "How It's Possible for an Ordinary Person to Lift a Car."

8. Josh Clark, "How Can Adrenaline Help You Lift a 3,500-Pound Car?," How Stuff Works, https://entertainment.howstuffworks.com/arts/circus-arts/adrenaline -strength1.htm.

to courage, resolution, and determination. We normally use only a small percentage of our strength capabilities. But an adrenaline rush can transform a timid weakling into a heroic Hercules.

Here is the point regarding the wonder worked by giving encouragement. I'm certainly not suggesting that encouragement biologically stimulates the hypothalamus and in turn explodes a literal adrenaline rush propelling to excellent performance. But I certainly am claiming an analogy. Encouragement is in many ways like adrenaline.

My thesis in a nutshell: What adrenaline is able to chemically and physiologically do for the body, encouragement is able to emotionally and psychologically do for the soul. Encouragement can transform a person's spirit. Wise people know it and tap into it.

Encouragement Strengthens

The apostle Paul knew the exhilarating power of encouragement. Under the inspiration of the Holy Spirit, he prescribed that Christians frequently help each other in running the race of the Christian life with a steady diet of encouragement. To do so he used the Greek word *parakaleo*, which translated literally means "encourage"; some Scripture translators use the word *comfort*. In 1 Thessalonians 5:11, Paul writes, "Therefore, comfort [literally, encourage] each other, and edify [literally, build up or strengthen] one another, just as you also are doing."

Comfort, or *encourage* (*parakaleo*), in this context means "to urge with uplifting words," "to console," "to cheer up especially in times of discouragement and sorrow." Notice the context. A number of the church members in Thessalonica had lost loved ones to death (see 1 Thess. 4:13) since Paul had departed. These church members were grieving and prone to despair, fearing that their loved ones' deaths that occurred before Jesus's second coming would disqualify them from participating in the forever salvation Christ's appearing will bring. Into these discouraged souls, Paul injects good news: "For this we say to you by the word of the

Lord, that we who are alive and remain until the coming of the Lord will by no means precede those who are asleep.... The dead in Christ will rise first. Then we who are alive and remain shall be caught up together with them in the clouds to meet the Lord in the air. And thus we shall always be with the Lord" (4:15–17). This is good news that brings joy-filled rapture. We'll see our dead brothers and sisters again and forever bask with them in the Lord's presence! J. Philip Arthur comments, "Though the present seemed threatening, the future could not look brighter. Paul was aware that his friends already appreciated how important it was to strengthen those who were feeling discouraged. Let them go on from this good beginning; let each of them excel in the business of fortifying and building up his or her brothers and sisters."[9] So let us abound in this grace of encouraging one another.

Some time ago, as a pastor slugging it out in bleak church-life difficulties, I found myself emotionally worn and weary. I was exhausted like a heavyweight boxer in the late rounds. Then I got an email from a dear woman in the church: "Pastor, I thought you'd like to know that I was just talking with Sue. She told me that after your sermon on Sunday night, her husband went home and said that after hearing your message he had to spend some time alone with God. He stayed in his bedroom alone for a long time and came out noticeably refreshed and changed."

That note of encouragement had such an effect on me! I was a down-for-the-count boxer who received smelling salts and was now invigorated, enthused, enlivened, energized, strengthened, and exhilarated. My outlook was radically changed. George M. Adams has said, "Encouragement is oxygen for the soul." It was adrenaline to me.

---

9. J. Philip Arthur, *Patience of Hope: 1 and 2 Thessalonians Simply Explained* (Darlington, England: Evangelical Press, 1996), 178.

Encouragement Gladdens

The book of Proverbs is full of encouragement to be encouraging: "Anxiety in the heart of man causes depression, but a good word makes it glad" (12:25). The word *glad* here in the Hebrew is *sameh*. It is the same Hebrew word used in 1 Samuel 11:9 when the Israelite city of Jabesh Gilead was being surrounded and threatened by Nahash, king of Ammon. This bully pledged that the only way he would let the citizens survive is if they would agree to let him gouge out all their right eyes (11:2). But then the people received a "good word," an encouraging one. Their new king Saul had heard about this bully and was angry about the threat, so he assembled an army of sixty thousand Israelites and began marching toward Jabesh Gilead. He sent a message to the fretting, eye-twitching town: "'Tomorrow, by the time the sun is hot, you shall have help.' Then the messengers came and reported it to the men of Jabesh, and they were glad [*sameh*]" (11:9). Their anxieties were calmed and their hearts revived by the "good word" of encouragement.

Parents may be concerned about the condition of their freshman son hundreds of miles away from home on an unfamiliar college campus. "How's he doing? Has he gotten in with the wrong crowd? Is he spiritually okay?" Then comes a Sunday night phone call from friends: "We are on our way home from visiting our daughter at the campus. We saw your David there. He was in the cafeteria surrounded by this great group of guys. He stood right up, greeted us, and introduced us to his friends. Looks like he's really thriving!" The anxious parental heart begins singing. Gary Brady comments practically on Proverbs 12:25: "It has staggered me on occasions to find myself in a thunderous mood, only for it to be dispelled by a mere smile or pleasantry from someone."[10]

---

10. Gary Brady, *Heavenly Wisdom: Proverbs Simply Explained* (Darlington, England: Evangelical Press, 2003), 346.

Encouragement Fattens

Solomon educates us: "The light of the eyes rejoices the heart, and a good report makes the bones healthy [literally, puts fat on the bones]" (Prov. 15:30). Today, things that are fat seem unhealthy. But in Old Testament times, when poverty meant malnutrition, a little pudginess meant prosperity. We understand that financially and emotionally too. When we are burdened with sorrow, we can lose our appetites, even become gaunt looking, and lose significant weight. If a spouse dies, the surviving partner may need to be prodded to eat something to keep up strength. The idea of putting fat on the bones refers to a heart at peace and full of joy. Derek Kidner has titled Proverbs 15:30 "Tonic." He writes, "*The light of the eyes* may perhaps refer to the radiant face of a friend (16:15); if so, the two lines of the proverb will be speaking of the heartwarming effect that persons and facts respectively can bring."[11]

Medical studies reveal that "enhanced patient expectations through positive information about the treatment of the illness, while providing support or reassurance significantly influenced health outcomes."[12] In other words, a physician's sharing positive feedback with a cancer patient gives a significant physiological boost to the patient.

A few years ago, a young man from our church was finishing his college degree. Stressed about his future, he paced in his home, filled with anxious concerns. With nothing certain for his professional career on the horizon, he felt hopeless and bleak. But then the phone rang, and the voice at the other end excitedly said, "Congratulations, Matt! You've been hired on to the White House staff of George W. Bush!" That good and encouraging word

---

11. Derek Kidner, *Proverbs: An Introduction and Commentary*, Tyndale Old Testament Commentaries, vol. 17 (Downers Grove, Ill.: InterVarsity Press, 2008), 117.

12. David Kernick, "Context and Health Outcomes," *The Lancet* 357, no. 9273 (June 23, 2001), https://www.thelancet.com/journals/lancet/article/PIIS0140-6736(00)05154-0/fulltext.

transformed the young man's determination and resolution from hopeless to Hercules, from scrawny to strength.

Encouragement Sweetens

Solomon again enlightens us: "Pleasant words are like a honeycomb, sweetness to the soul and health to the bones" (Prov. 16:24). George Lawson explains: "Words that convey proper counsels and consolations to persons in complexity and distress are pleasant and medicinal like honey from the comb. They revive the drooping spirit and strengthen the feeble knees."[13]

In 1 Samuel 14, King Saul's son Jonathan was fighting a marathon battle against the Philistines. Hour after hour he fought through the day, to the point of hunger and near exhaustion. He came to a forest where there was honey on the ground, and "he stretched out the end of the rod that was in his hand and dipped it in a honeycomb, and put his hand to his mouth; and his countenance [eyes] brightened" (v. 27). That honey had the effect of encouraging and pleasant words.

It is reported that in 1521, as Martin Luther was walking to the assembly room of the Diet at Worms, a noted German military commander, George Von Frundsberg, touched him on the shoulder and said, "My little monk, thou hast today a march and a struggle to go through such as neither I nor other great captains have seen in our most bloody battles; but if thy cause be just, go forward in God's name; he will not forsake thee."[14] This was a sweet balm to Luther's trembling heart, an exhilarating word of encouragement for his fainting frame.

---

13. George Lawson, *Commentary on Proverbs* (Grand Rapids: Kregel, 1993), 247.

14. Heinrich Boehmer, Carl Frederick Huth, and William Koepchen, *Luther in Light of Recent Research* (New York: Christian Herald, 1916), 50.

Encouragement Enlivens

Solomon again instructs us: "Death and life are in the power of the tongue, and those who love it will eat its fruit" (Prov. 18:21). We say, "Sticks and stones may break my bones, but words will never hurt me." But that is not really true. Words can pack the punch of a baseball bat. Ray Ortlund comments on Proverbs 18:21: "The tongue can kill—literally. I heard about a woman in Los Angeles who took her own life. All she wrote in her suicide note was this: 'They said.'"[15]

Ortlund expanded on this when he was interviewed for an *Ask Pastor John* (Piper) broadcast:

> We figure out as we go through life…who we are by the ping-backs we get from other people. We go to the Bible for the big question, "Who is humanity?" But when it comes to the smaller question, "Who am I within that humanity?" we have to notice how other people are responding to us and what they are saying to us, especially what they say to us about us. And impressions that we pick up from other people by their words can be life-giving or they can be life-depleting….
>
> We can by grace, in obedience to the Bible, to the glory of God breathe life into one another. Romans 12:10 says, "Outdo one another in showing honor."… So we have, for example, in our men's ministry…what we call honor time…. We open it up and guys will say, "Well, here is how I see Christ in you. Last Tuesday when I faced this challenge, you stepped out of your way at great inconvenience to yourself and you helped me. I saw Christ in you and I honor you for that." And typically, when I throw that open, immediately guys start speaking, and it is hard to shut it down.[16]

Larry Crabb, well-known Christian counselor, author, and speaker, tells of the humiliating stuttering problems he had as a

---

15. Raymond C. Ortlund, *Proverbs: Wisdom That Works,* Preaching the Word (Wheaton, Ill.: Crossway, 2012), 134.

16. Raymond C. Ortlund, "Why Gossip Destroys," *Ask Pastor John,* Desiring God, March 31, 2015, https://www.desiringgod.org/interviews/why-gossip-destroys.

youngster. In ninth grade he was elected president of the junior high student body. The principal called him on stage for his acceptance speech in front of several hundred fellow students.[17] He stuttered his way through the speech and decided then and there that public speaking was not for him.

A short time later, at his home church, Larry felt compelled to stand and spontaneously lead the congregation in prayer. He remembers that he was again paralyzed with stage fright and recalls, "I found my theology becoming confused to the point of heresy. I remember thanking the Father for hanging on the cross and praising Christ for triumphantly bringing the Spirit from the grave. Stuttering throughout, I finally thought of the word *Amen* (perhaps the first evidence of the Spirit's leading), said it, and sat down. I recall staring at the floor, too embarrassed to look around, and solemnly vowing never again to pray or speak aloud in front of a group." Crabb's ministry aspirations were dead. He scrambled for the door, hoping to avoid anyone who might want to correct his faulty theology. He writes about what happened when an older man pulled him aside and spoke to him:

> "Larry," he said, "there's one thing I want you to know. Whatever you do for the Lord, I'm behind you one thousand percent." Then he walked away. Even as I write these words, my eyes fill with tears. Those words were life words. They had power. They reached deep into my being. My resolve never again to speak publicly weakened instantly.
>
> Since the day those words were spoken, God has led me into a ministry in which I regularly address and pray before crowds of all sizes. I do it without stuttering. I love it. Not only death, but also life lies in the power of the tongue.[18]

Like an adrenaline shot to the body, encouragement can act as a powerful and enlivening tonic to the soul.

---

17. Larry Crabb and Dan B. Allender, *Encouragement: The Unexpected Power of Building Others Up* (Grand Rapids: Zondervan, 2013), 26.

18. Crabb and Allender, *Encouragement*, 27.

2

The Obligation of
ENCOURAGEMENT

It does people good to be told how highly we value them.
There is many a Christian man and woman who would do
better if now and then someone would speak a kindly word
to them, and let them know that they had done well.

—Charles Spurgeon

In August 2014, a nine-year-old American girl was traveling on
board a transatlantic United Airlines flight from Dublin, Ireland, to
Newark, New Jersey. Less than two hours into the flight, the young
passenger became ill, apparently suffering an allergic reaction.
Her face puffed up. She began displaying the suffocating distress
of anaphylactic shock: dizziness, labored breathing, swelling of the
tongue and breathing passages, blueness of skin. Things got desperate, and medical professionals on board feared a fatal outcome.

But the airline crew was equipped with an EpiPen®—an
emergency shot of adrenaline. The term EpiPen® comes from the
medicinal term for adrenaline, which is *epinephrine*. The injec-
tor looks like a small pen, and it is often carried by children who
are allergic to peanuts or bee stings. It has a needle at its tip and
is sealed by a black plastic cap. Inside is a glass cartridge contain-
ing adrenaline. When the adrenaline is injected into the thigh
of an allergic-reaction victim, it transforms the body. The heart
is stimulated, increasing the pulse rate. Blood vessels constrict.
Blood pressure increases. Smooth muscles relax in the lungs,

reducing wheezing and improving breathing. Death is averted. Health returns.[1]

Although the flight and its 169 passengers were forced to make a dramatic U-turn and return immediately to Dublin, the story's ending was a happy one for the nine-year-old American girl. She was rushed to a Dublin hospital and was given a clean bill of health. The shot of adrenaline saved her life.

But sadly, in December of the previous year, a fourteen-year-old Dublin girl, Emma Sloan, was not as fortunate when she lost her life. Just days after Christmas, she suffered an allergic reaction to a restaurant nut sauce. She had forgotten her prescription, and the pharmacy refused to give her and her mother the lifesaving EpiPen®. She suffocated to death for lack of adrenaline.[2]

What's true in the physical realm is strikingly true in the emotional-spiritual realm. People are vulnerable to the suffocation of extreme discouragement, and we are solemnly obligated to give them shots of encouragement when it is within our power to deliver.

Do unto Others

Many Bible passages remind us that our words have nearly incalculable power:

> Death and life are in the power of the tongue. (Prov. 18:21)

> Let no corrupt word proceed out of your mouth, but what is good for necessary edification, that it may impart grace to the hearers. (Eph. 4:29)

Being encouraging is an obligation we have to fellow human beings, especially to our Christian brothers and sisters. The writer to the Hebrews instructs his audience, "Let us consider one another

---

1. "EpiPen (Adrenaline)," Netdoctor, June 16, 2014, http://www.netdoctor.co.uk/medicines/allergy-and-asthma/news/a6668/epipen-adrenaline/.

2. "US Bound Plane Forced to Return to Dublin after Nut Allergy Emergency," IrishCentral.com, August 6, 2014, http://www.irishcentral.com/news/US-bound-plane-forced-to-return-to-Dublin-after-nut-allergy-emergency.html.

in order to stir up love and good works, not forsaking the assembling of ourselves together, as is the manner of some, but exhorting [encouraging] one another, and so much the more as you see the Day approaching" (10:24–25).

If you saw a child in a restaurant with a swollen face, gasping for air, and you had an EpiPen® in your pocket, you wouldn't think of passing by without seeking to deliver a life-giving shot of adrenaline. But some of us pass by our neighbors and dear ones daily, habitually neglecting to inject the encouragement we have within our power to deliver. Scripture warns us against this:

> Do not withhold good from those to whom it is due,
> When it is in the power of your hand to do so. (Prov. 3:27)

> Therefore, to him who knows to do good and does not do it,
> to him it is sin. (James 4:17)

You may ask, "But how do I know if someone needs encouragement?" S. Truett Cathy, founder of the booming Chick-fil-A restaurant chain, helps us here: "How do you identify someone who needs encouragement? That person is breathing."

That is not really news to any of us. We all know what it is to be emotionally gasping for air, feeling psychologically suffocated by discouragement, downcast by disappointments, and having a bleak outlook on life. Maybe I didn't get that job I had hoped for. Maybe my children's problems are like a heavy weight pressing down on my chest. Maybe I'm staring at myself in the mirror, thinking that I don't have a single true friend who really cares about me. Discouragement is epidemic. People everywhere are weary and "heavy laden" (Matt. 11:28).

We are all tempted to despair and depression—even the sturdiest of us. Philip Ryken, president of Wheaton College, gave a striking chapel message in September 2014. It was titled "Nobody Knows the Trouble I've Seen." He spoke candidly to an audience full of discouragement-prone undergraduates about his own experience just a few months earlier:

It was the spring semester of the academic year, and I was in trouble. Over the course of long weeks that stretched into months, I fell deeper and deeper into discouragement until eventually I wondered whether I had the will to live. I'm talking about me, not somebody else.... I was in a downward spiral. I said to myself: "You know, I understand why people would kill themselves." A few days after that I started to wonder how I would end it all.... It wasn't a thought I wanted to have, but Satan was after me. He was tempting me. Things were moving in a bad direction, and at the rate they were going, who knows how long it would be before I was in real danger.[3]

Really? The renowned Christian leader, speaker, and writer Philip Ryken was suffocating under the burden of discouragement? He was struggling just like me? Did anyone know this when they crossed paths with him on campus that spring semester of 2014? The apostle Paul reminds us that no one is exempt: "No temptation has overtaken you except such as is common to man" (1 Cor. 10:13).

I was recently going through a difficult season of ministry as a pastor in my church. I'd been at my post for over twenty-one years and began wondering if my time as a pastor at this church was coming to an end. I began to think that my voice had become like a redundant waterfall that makes a refreshing and invigorating sound when you first move near it but can become monotonous and nearly unnoticeable after you've lived there a long time. I purposefully went away for a few Sundays to clear my head. After I was back in the pulpit a few weeks, a mature, dear woman in our congregation pulled me aside, got my full attention, and said, "You know, Pastor Mark, listening to visiting pastors' preaching is fine, but it is so good to have you back. No one knows us like you do. We are so thankful for your ministry." That woman didn't know it,

---

3. Philip Ryken, "Nobody Knows the Trouble I've Seen," March 17, 2015, in Wheaton College Chapel Services 2014–2015, podcast, https://itunes.apple.com /us/podcast/chapel-services-2014–2015-audio/id977356855?mt=2.

but she had just shot me with an EpiPen®! I was a new man. She could have just passed by that day and said nothing, but she didn't.

Timely encouragement doesn't necessarily have to be anything dramatic. Recently Sally, a mother of four young children, told me of an EpiPen® she freshly got stuck with. She has felt overwhelmed with caring for the basic needs of her little ones, and she wishes she had more tender one-on-one time with them. She feels so negligent. On her blue days, she fears she's unleashing a herd of dangerous delinquents into an unsuspecting world. But last week a sweet grandmother who was visiting in the neighborhood ventured down the street to knock on Sally's door and inform Sally that her firstborn son is the kindest boy in the neighborhood. "He actually cares deeply about his little playmates! It shows in the way he talks to them and treats them. You should be very proud of him." These simple words were new life to a fainting mommy!

Yes, we are solemnly obligated to be encouragers. Jesus reminded His disciples, "Just as you want men to do to you, you also do to them likewise" (Luke 6:31). C. H. Spurgeon, the famous London preacher, wrote, "It does people good to be told how highly we value them. There is many a Christian man and woman who would do better if now and then someone would speak a kindly word to them, and let them know that they had done well."[4]

Pour Out Praise

One Sunday afternoon we were hosting a number of college students at our dining room table. Colorful comments were volleyed back and forth between passing the potatoes and pouring the gravy. Then Jerry shouted over the hubbub, "Hey everybody, last week Chris was awarded a premedical scholarship from the biology department!" Chris's face beamed, and there were pats on the back all around. That was beautiful. A passage in Proverbs tells us we are obligated to do two things: first, don't brag, and second, do

---

4. C. H. Spurgeon, sermon 2233, in *Metropolitan Tabernacle Pulpit* (1891; repr., Pasadena, Tex.: Pilgrim Publications, 1969–1980), 37:618.

praise—others: "Let another man praise you, and not your own mouth; a stranger, and not your own lips" (27:2). And that is what had just happened at my dining room table.

A husband is solemnly obligated to encourage his godly wife with commending praise both publicly at the city gates and privately:

> Her children rise up and call her blessed;
> Her husband also, and he praises her:
> "Many daughters have done well,
> But you excel them all."
> Charm is deceitful and beauty is passing,
> But a woman who fears the LORD, she shall be praised.
> Give her of the fruit of her hands,
> And let her own works praise her in the gates.
> (Prov. 31:28–31)

Sadly, many precious women's spirits have shriveled up, and they are withering away on the inside because their husbands don't give them well-deserved praise and encouragement. "Oh, I encourage her!" a husband may say. But maybe he is stingy and uses an eyedropper to deliver praise when he should use a garden hose.

Act Like an Angel

It is our holy obligation to generously encourage one another. Jesus taught us in the third petition of the Lord's Prayer to pray,

> Your kingdom come,
> Your will be done,
> On earth as it is in heaven. (Matt. 6:10)

The Westminster Shorter Catechism correctly summarizes the significance of this petition: "We pray that God, by his grace, would make us able and willing to know, obey and submit to his will in all things, as the angels do in heaven." And a chief trait of angels is that they are great encouragers. We see that as they announce Christ's birth to shepherds tending their flocks at night. Notice all the italicized expressions of encouragement in this passage:

Now there were in the same country shepherds living out in the fields, keeping watch over their flock by night. And behold, an angel of the Lord stood before them, and the glory of the Lord shone around them, and they were greatly afraid. Then the angel said to them, "Do not be afraid, for behold, I bring you *good tidings of great joy* which will be to all people. For *there is born to you this day in the city of David a Savior, who is Christ the Lord.* And this will be the sign to you: You will find a Babe wrapped in swaddling cloths, lying in a manger."

And suddenly there was with the angel a multitude of the heavenly host praising God and saying:

"Glory to God in the highest,

And *on earth peace, goodwill toward men!*" (Luke 2:8–14)

Richard Sibbes writes about angels' encouraging and cheering ministry to people, especially in announcing the birth of Christ:

God uses angels…for the further demonstration of His goodness. He is so diffusive of goodness, He will have a multitude of creatures that they may be a means to diffuse His goodness: angels to the church, and the church to others…. We may see by the way that for one Christian to confirm and comfort another, it is the work of an angel, it is an angelic work; for one man to discourage another, it is the work of a devil. When Christ was in agony, the angels appeared to comfort Him (Luke 22:43)…. We love the examples of great, noted persons. Here you have an example above yourselves, the example of angels.[5]

The author of Hebrews points out the encouraging task of angels: "Are they [angels] not all ministering spirits sent forth to minister [serve] for those who will inherit salvation?" (1:14). As angels serve us, so we ought to serve one another.

---

5. Richard Sibbes, *Works of Richard Sibbes*, ed. Alexander Balloch Grosart (Edinburgh: Banner of Truth, 2001), 6:320–22.

Centuries earlier, a Midianite-fearing, knee-knocking Gideon got the same treatment from the Angel of the Lord. He called Gideon, "mighty man of valor":

> Now the Angel of the LORD came and sat under the terebinth tree which was in Ophrah, which belonged to Joash the Abiezrite, while his son Gideon threshed wheat in the winepress, in order to hide it from the Midianites. And the Angel of the LORD appeared to him, and said to him, "The LORD is with you, you mighty man of valor!" (Judg. 6:11–12).

It is encouraging and transforming when others see things in us that we don't see in ourselves and tell us about it. It is angelic. Yes, we are to profoundly take our cues from angels as we seek to do God's will on earth as it is done in heaven (Matt. 6:10). That means we are to have a peculiarly compassionate eye for our neighbors, sensitively aware that they are constitutionally weak and frail, just like Gideon and we are. We all have a holy obligation to speak true, strengthening, and emboldening words of encouragement to people with whom we cross paths.

Be Aware Constantly

Larry Crabb is right when he says that "encouragers must constantly remind themselves that the people with whom they rub shoulders are facing problems in life which, but for the grace of God, are ultimately overwhelming. It is this conscious awareness that can give encouraging power to even the most trivial conversation."[6]

Mary Beeke writes, "I heard a story once of a boy who was so depressed that he decided to end his life by jumping off a bridge in New York. He left a note saying that if anyone along the way would smile or speak a kind word to him, he would not go through with his plan. Nobody did. So he did. I have always hoped this story was fictitious. I don't know, but it has spurred me on to observe

---

6. Crabb and Allender, *Encouragement*, 96.

people and, if the situation is appropriate, to smile or say an encouraging word."[7]

What's true about adrenaline in the physical realm is strikingly true about encouragement in the spiritual realm. The world is a cursed, dangerous, and unfriendly place, full of bee stings, nut sauces, tragedies, and disappointments. EpiPens® and timely words can rescue lives. People are vulnerable to the suffocation of extreme discouragement, and we are solemnly obligated to give them shots of encouragement when it is within our power to deliver.

---

7. Mary Beeke, *The Law of Kindness: Serving with Heart and Hands* (Grand Rapids: Reformation Heritage Books, 2007), 182.

3

Some Direct Expressions of
ENCOURAGEMENT

A church (like a culture) that does not recognize the sacrifices of its own for the sake of the gospel makes a big mistake.
—R. Kent Hughes

The apostle Paul knew personally what it was to be a dejected outcast in need of some encouragement. In Acts 9, when he was still the wolf-like Saul, he savingly met the Lord Jesus on the road to Damascus, where he had planned on spending his time arresting and persecuting Christian saints. But Saul became Paul. So instead, he spent his time in Damascus witnessing to and evangelizing Jewish sinners. And he was no more popular among the Damascus Jews as an evangelist than he would have been among the Damascus Christians as a persecutor. Paul's surprised Jewish audience hated him and his gospel. Though Paul "increased all the more in strength" (v. 22) due to God's amazing, strengthening grace, he actually became a hunted man: "Now after many days were past, the Jews plotted to kill him. But their plot became known to Saul. And they watched the gates day and night, to kill him. Then the disciples took him by night and let him down through the wall in a large basket" (vv. 23–25).

That is discouraging! Paul's first ministry endeavors are preserved by a report marking zero converts and a conspiracy to lynch him. How humiliating it must have been for him to be forced to flee by stealth of darkness, to have friends lower him over the wall by a rope while he was curled up in a basket! In 2 Corinthians

11:23–25 and 30–33, Paul associates this great escape experience with weakness, ranking right up there with his being beaten, lashed, and stoned. Probably he traveled on foot southward in a dazed and dejected condition. Ananias had prophesied that Paul was to be God's "chosen vessel" (Acts 9:15) and that on regaining his sight, Paul would be "filled with the Holy Spirit" (v. 17). But his ministry seemingly had little effect. He probably approached Jerusalem emotionally fragile, despite his ministry having had the effect God intended it to have—he proved to Jews that Jesus is the Christ.

But among the Christians there he found no soothing ointment. Imagine how crestfallen the vulnerable fledgling disciple Paul might have been when he faced harsh rejection from the mother church: "And when Saul had come to Jerusalem, he tried to join the disciples; but they were all afraid of him, and did not believe that he was a disciple" (Acts 9:26). They weren't friendly like Ananias and the other disciples in Damascus. Instead, the Jerusalem believers were suspicious, shunning, and skeptical. This probably left Paul disheartened, spiritually and emotionally. But then came the man known for always carrying around EpiPens® of encouragement. His name was Barnabas, "which is translated Son of Encouragement" (4:36). "But Barnabas took him and brought him to the apostles. And he declared to them how he had seen the Lord on the road, and that He had spoken to him, and how he had preached boldly at Damascus in the name of Jesus" (9:27).

Barnabas most likely encouraged Paul by publicly affirming his spiritual heroism in Damascus. This well-timed, loving encouragement turned the tide in the church, resulting in Paul being highly esteemed and in all likelihood personally resuscitated. I don't think Paul ever forgot this lesson—and many more—from Barnabas, who became his long-term ministry companion. Barnabas's impress of encouragement is all over Paul's letters. Eventually, Paul himself became a man known for always carrying around EpiPens® as well.

Notice a few snapshots of Paul's interpersonal handling of friends, coworkers, brothers, and sisters in his final friendly greetings to the church in Rome in Romans 16:

I commend to you Phoebe our sister, who is a servant of the church in Cenchrea, that you may receive her in the Lord in a manner worthy of the saints...for indeed she has been a helper of many and of myself also.

Greet Priscilla and Aquila, my fellow workers in Christ Jesus, who risked their own necks for my life, to whom not only I give thanks, but also all the churches of the Gentiles....

Greet Mary, who labored much for us....

Greet Apelles, approved in Christ....

Greet Tryphena and Tryphosa, who have labored in the Lord....

Greet Rufus, chosen [a choice man, NASB] in the Lord, and his mother and mine....

Greet one another with a holy kiss. The churches of Christ greet you. (vv. 1–4, 6, 10, 12, 13, 16)

This correspondence pulses with multiple expressions of encouragement. It reminds me of occasions when I've witnessed faithful pastors imitating the Barnabas-like apostle Paul. It is always enjoyable after preaching at a sister church on a Sunday morning when a pastor personally introduces me to many members of his precious flock. What a joy it has been to experience the blessed uplift exchanged when the pastor tells an affectionate and humorous story about Mr. Smith and gives a high compliment to Mrs. Jones. He shares warm anecdotes and laughter with various members. He offers high praise for the dedication of a deacon and a tender word of appreciation for the selflessness of the church secretary. Like Paul, such a pastor blows in a surge of updraft under the wings of his people.

Let's consider a dozen stock expressions of encouragement we would all do well to employ. Then we'll expand on these expressions further as the book unfolds.

Commendation

To *commend* is to heartily express approval for a job well done in the hearing of the one being praised in such a way that others come to trust and esteem that individual. That is just what Paul did in paving the way for a dear sister in Christ: "I commend to you Phoebe our sister, who is a servant of the church in Cenchrea.... Indeed she has been a helper of many and of myself also" (Rom. 16:1–2).

At ten years old, I went alone to the city park early on a spring Saturday morning to try out for a position on my neighborhood's Little League team. I had told my mom that I didn't want to go. I was intimidated and paralyzed with the insecure feeling of being an incompetent nobody. Even my otherwise ever-present big brothers weren't with me. But then my previous year's minor team coach came by the field and shouted to the majors coach that I was the man for the shortstop position for the upcoming year. He said I had a great bat, glove, and arm. Those few words of commendation opened up for me a wonderful door of opportunity, transforming me and my performance that day. I started at shortstop all that year.

Albert Mohler refreshingly gave commendation during one of his *Thinking in Public* interviews. In conversing with former *Newsweek* religion editor Kenneth L. Woodward, Mohler said,

> In closing, I want to tell you something as a word of appreciation. If I ever have the opportunity to write a memoir, and I honestly do hope to do so at some point, I have a collection of books just to remind myself of models I'd like to incorporate in such a work. And your book, *Getting Religion*, is one of those books. I think you tell the story so incredibly well. I just wanted you to know that I greatly appreciated that.[1]

Listeners to the broadcast can hear the change in Woodward's voice after that "well done" from Mohler. He began speaking with refreshed energy. The effect was audibly electric.

---

1. Albert Mohler, "Getting American Religion: A Conversation with Former *Newsweek* Religion Editor Kenneth L. Woodward," *Thinking in Public*, AlbertMohler .com, December 5, 2016, http://albertmohler.com/2016/12/05/getting-american -religion/.

Boasting

To boast or brag with pride about your own achievements is unattractive, but to boast in the outstanding performances of others is splendid. Proverbs 27:2 says, "Let another man praise you, and not your own mouth." Paul often did it—within earshot of the objects of his boasting. He boasted in the heroism of Priscilla and Aquila, who had "risked their own necks" for his life (Rom. 16:4). Maybe Paul was alluding to the brave valor they displayed in shielding him from the assassination-minded Jews who dragged him before Gallio in Corinth (Acts 18:9–17) or in sheltering him from the murderous stadium mob in Ephesus (19:28–31).

Paul also boasted about the robust spirituality of the Corinthians:

> Great is my boldness of speech toward you, great is my boasting on your behalf. I am filled with comfort. I am exceedingly joyful in all our tribulation. (2 Cor. 7:4)

> For if in anything I have boasted to him about you, I am not ashamed. But as we spoke all things to you in truth, even so our boasting to Titus was found true. (7:14)

> Therefore show to them, and before the churches, the proof of your love and of our boasting on your behalf. (8:24)

> For I know your willingness, about which I boast of you to the Macedonians, that Achaia was ready a year ago; and your zeal has stirred up the majority. Yet I have sent the brethren, lest our boasting of you should be in vain in this respect, that, as I said, you may be ready. (9:2–3)

And of the Thessalonians he boasted:

> We are bound to thank God always for you, brethren, as it is fitting, because your faith grows exceedingly, and the love of every one of you all abounds toward each other, so that we ourselves boast of you among the churches of God for your patience and faith in all your persecutions and tribulations that you endure. (2 Thess. 1:3–4)

These words weren't intended to puff up the recipients with pride, but to spur them on with inspiration. How about tweeting this? "My roommate Terry is graduating summa cum laude, while almost single-handedly carrying not-so-smart me through organic chemistry! #bestever."

Approval

"Greet Apelles, approved in Christ" (Rom. 16:10). To receive confirmation that we are on the right track and accepted by wise friends or colleagues can be empowering. That is approval.

The young inventor Henry Ford first met the famous inventor Thomas Edison at a convention. Someone pointed out Ford as "a young man who has made a gas car." Edison spoke for some time with Ford about this automobile idea, and suddenly Edison enthusiastically banged his fist down on the table, exclaiming, "You have it! Your car is self-contained and carries its own power plant." Later, Ford reflected on this encounter and wrote, "That bang on the table was worth worlds to me. No man up to then had given me any encouragement. I had hoped that I was headed right. Sometimes I knew that I was, sometimes I only wondered, but here, all at once and out of a clear sky, the greatest inventive genius in the world had given me complete approval."[2]

Though I am by no means a fan of Walt Whitman or many of his unbiblical views, he became a legendary nineteenth-century American poet. For years few readers expressed any interest in his poems. He was fainting. Then came the EpiPen®. It is preserved in the Library of Congress. It came in the form of a letter expressing admiration for his then little-known book of poetry titled *Leaves of Grass*. It read, "Dear Sir, I am not blind to the worth of the wonderful gift of 'Leaves of Grass.' I find it the most extraordinary piece of wit and wisdom that America has yet contributed. I am very happy in reading it, as great power makes us happy.... I greet you at the

---

2. John C. Maxwell, *Encouragement Changes Everything: Bless and Be Blessed* (Nashville: Thomas Nelson, 2008), 110.

beginning of a great career."[3] It was signed by Ralph Waldo Emerson. Whitman kept the entire gushing five-page handwritten note of appreciation as a treasure that he often pulled out and reviewed when fainting along the exhausting way of an oft-discouraged writer. That is why it remains on display at the Library of Congress. It launched a legend.

Report

Sharing a verbal account of another person's achievement, accomplishment, or heroism can give a shot of epinephrine to that person and his or her loved ones: "Greet Rufus, chosen [a choice man, NASB] in the Lord, and his mother and mine" (Rom. 16:13). Here, Paul takes the time to extend his apostolic approval to Rufus as "a choice man in the Lord." But he also has an eye toward Rufus's mother, who would be greatly encouraged by the report of her son being highly esteemed: "A wise son makes a glad father, but a foolish son is the grief of his mother" (Prov. 10:1). Proverbs 15:30 tells us that "a good report makes the bones healthy." Paul's report of Rufus's honorable stature no doubt brought delight and thankful satisfaction to Rufus's mother.

As a board member of a Christian school, I received from a mother of a middle school student this note of appreciation that demonstrates the power of a good report: "I got a call from my son's teacher during a recent break from school. She was grading papers and had just finished grading my son's writing assignment. She called on her day off from school to share with me what he had written because she knew that, as a mom, it was going to make my day. And it did."

Paul found that the kingdom heroism of Epaphroditus was worth reporting to the church at Philippi, and he used a significant part of his letter to make sure Epaphroditus received his due:

---

3. Ralph Waldo Emerson to Walt Whitman. A transcription of this letter is available on the website of the Library of Congress, https://www.loc.gov/exhibits/whitman/0017-trans.html.

Yet I considered it necessary to send to you Epaphroditus, my brother, fellow worker, and fellow soldier, but your messenger and the one who ministered to my need; since he was longing for you all, and was distressed because you had heard that he was sick. For indeed he was sick almost unto death; but God had mercy on him, and not only on him but on me also, lest I should have sorrow upon sorrow. Therefore I sent him the more eagerly, that when you see him again you may rejoice, and I may be less sorrowful. Receive him therefore in the Lord with all gladness, and hold such men in esteem; because for the work of Christ he came close to death, not regarding his life, to supply what was lacking in your service toward me. (Phil. 2:25–30)

Paul had been thrown into prison in Rome, a system that didn't provide food, clothing, or medical care for its inmates. The church at Philippi took up an offering and sent Epaphroditus with a sizable money bag and a servant's heart on an eight-hundred-mile adventure to Rome. Along the way, Epaphroditus was hit with a life-threatening illness, but he eventually made it to Paul and faithfully delivered the goods and the service. Upon returning home to Philippi, Epaphroditus was decorated with Paul's appreciative report of his selfless heroism.

Kent Hughes comments on how the United States failed to recognize the heroism of Vietnam veterans when they returned from the battlefields. He writes, "A church (like a culture) that does not recognize the sacrifices of its own for the sake of the gospel makes a big mistake. And the wise apostle simply would not let that happen.... Epaphroditus had put on the mind of Christ..., taking on the humble life of an unsung servant. The Philippians needed to see the young man for the man he was and receive him as such."[4]

---

4. R. Kent Hughes, *Philippians: The Fellowship of the Gospel*, Preaching the Word (Wheaton, Ill.: Crossway, 2007), 114–16.

Paul refused to let Epaphroditus's heroism go unsung. In kind, we should make it a matter of conscience to sing the praise of others by reporting their exploits.

Name Recognition

We each feel more valued, respected, and important when someone remembers and uses our names. When someone who met you only once greets you by name, it is an invigorating breath of fresh air, in contrast to how you feel when a colleague or acquaintance you've spoken to occasionally seems unable to retrieve your name from his or her memory. Recognizing and using a person's name can deliver eye-brightening encouragement.

After my freshman year at a feeder junior high school, I went to the gym of the big high school for summer league basketball. For me, these were big-time initial tryouts. With all the guys there vying for only a few choice spots on the team, I felt small and insignificant, timid and lacking confidence. But during a drill, Head Coach Haskins shouted out, "Good job, Chanski!" He knew my name! Instantly, my play was transformed—emboldened and improved. A couple of weeks later, when Coach handed out the T-shirt summer uniforms, mine, unlike the other no-name sophomore shirts, had "Chanski" emblazoned on the back, just like the upper classmen. True, it didn't make me Michael Jordan, but the confidence it instilled made me play a lot better.

David had a fond attachment to his mighty men and made sure they were aware of his appreciation for their loyalty and acts of valor. The public mention of their names (along with the reporting of their deeds) was an important dimension of morale boosting. In 2 Samuel 23:8–39 the mighty men get their due. All thirty-seven are listed, as well as some of their accomplishments, including attacking the Philistines and defending a field of lentils from them, breaking through the Philistine camp to get water from the Bethlehem well for David, and striking down a lion in a pit on a snowy day. Could it be that in King David's Israel name recognition inspired battlefield performance?

Nehemiah did the same with his army of mighty Jerusalem wall rebuilders who together completed their daunting task in an unthinkable fifty-two days. Their construction exploits were heroic. In chapter 3, he painstakingly names the individual platoon leaders section by section and credits them specifically for their contributions to the rebuilt wall. I count no fewer than eighty names in this chapter. That is a lot of biblical ink spilled in mentioning names. And not an ounce of it is wasted or is without purpose. Every jot and tittle packs instruction. There is a lesson. The healthy prospects of name recognition inspired work performance. That was true in Nehemiah's generation and in generations yet to come.

Our Lord Jesus wonderfully and effectively made it a point to use people's names:

> And when Jesus came to the place, He looked up and saw him, and said to him, "*Zacchaeus*, make haste and come down, for today I must stay at your house." (Luke 19:5)

> Jesus said to her, "Woman, why are you weeping? Whom are you seeking?"
> She, supposing Him to be the gardener, said to Him, "Sir, if You have carried Him away, tell me where You have laid Him, and I will take Him away."
> Jesus said to her, "*Mary!*" (John 20:15–16)

> But go, tell His disciples—and *Peter*—that He is going before you into Galilee; there you will see Him, as He said to you. (Mark 16:7)

What a balm it must have been for Peter, who denied Jesus three times, to hear that Jesus had instructed the angel to provide a reunion invitation to him by name, despite his unworthiness. I imagine him asking the breathless women repeatedly, "Did he actually speak my name?"

John M. Yeager writes:

The power of naming came to light again for me last year when a fellow teacher at the Culver Academies told me that he thanked each student by name and shook each of their hands as they left class each day.... So, I decided to formally greet by name each of my students as they arrived at the classroom door. This brought back positive images of my third grade teacher, Mrs. Robinson, who was there every morning to greet me: "Good morning, John. What a nice shirt you are wearing!" When she was absent one day, it just wasn't the same.

I now stand at the classroom door and greet each student as they cross under the archway. A shake of the hand, a verbal greeting by name with eye contact welcomes them into a warm, inviting environment. "Good morning, Zack. Good to see you." "Hi Mary, I heard you got into your first choice for college." "Ben, I've heard you are doing a great job as lacrosse captain."[5]

Tim Keller recounted this experience for the Wheaton College chapel audience:

When I was a very unsure of myself person, thinking I wanted to go into the ministry, and wasn't sure I could make it, I met a guy, Edmund Clowney, who was an alumnus of Wheaton College. He was the president of Westminster Seminary. I heard him speak at a conference. I walked up and met him. Two years later, when I was really down in the dumps about my prospects, I heard he was speaking nearby. I went and afterwards I walked up, and I said, "Hello Dr. Clowney. I met you before. You don't remember me but I...." He said, "Oh, I know you." And he named me! He named me! And he said, "Let's go get a soda and talk, and find out what's going on in

---

5. John Yeager, "'I've Got a Name'—The Power of Positive Salutation," *Positive Psychology News* (blog), February 10, 2007, http://positivepsychologynews.com /news/john-yeager/2007021090.

your life." That just changed everything. He named me.... It was transformative.[6]

For good reason the apostle John concluded his third letter with these words: "Peace to you. Our friends greet you. Greet the friends by name" (v. 14). It is an encouraging, uncommon, and godly trait to know, remember, recognize, and call others by their names.

Cheering On

Cheering on is shouting out inspiring support to someone whose spirits may be flagging with a sense of weakness or hopelessness. Nehemiah cheered on his enemy-threatened and vulnerable-feeling coworkers as they rebuilt the walls of Jerusalem. When he saw the fear in his team's eyes, he rose to the occasion and gave a verbal boost to the nobles, officials, and the rest of the people: "Do not be afraid of them. Remember the Lord, great and awesome, and fight for your brethren, your sons, your daughters, your wives, and your houses" (Neh. 4:14). "We are doing a great work, and we can't come down" (see Neh. 6:3)!

Paul cheers on the battle-fatigued saints of Galatia in their critical kingdom labors: "And let us not grow weary while doing good, for in due season we shall reap if we do not lose heart" (Gal. 6:9). The surrounding great "cloud of witnesses" who cheer us on in our heavenly marathon race should consist of both dead saints and living ones (Heb. 12:1–2).

D. L. Moody persuaded his congregation to cheer one another on in spiritual challenges with this illustration:

> You have heard the story, I suppose, of the child who was rescued from the fire that was raging in a house away up in the fourth story. The child came to the window and as the flames were shooting up higher and higher, it cried out for help. A

6. Tim Keller, "Our Identity: The Christian Alternative to Late Modernity's Story," recorded at Wheaton College, 11/11/2015, https://www.youtube.com/watch?v=Ehw87PqTwKw.

fireman started up the ladder of the fire escape to rescue the child from its dangerous position. The wind swept the flames near him, and it was getting so hot that he wavered, and it looked as if he would have to return without the child. Thousands looked on, and their hearts quaked at the thought of the child having to perish in the fire, as it must do if the fireman did not reach it. Someone in the crowd cried, "Give him a cheer!" Cheer after cheer went up, and as the man heard them he gathered fresh courage. Up he went into the midst of the smoke and the fire, and brought down the child to safety.[7]

During the 2018 Winter Olympics, on countless occasions, the blue-clad South Korean skaters were pushed to personal record-breaking performances, enabling them to defeat more highly rated competitors. Why? The Olympics were held in Pyeongchang, South Korea, and the cheering home-nation crowd filling the arenas spurred the skaters on to previously unthinkable speeds. "It doesn't take much examination of the statistics to be able to confirm what was already fairly obvious to sports fans—the home team wins more often. This is particularly true of the Olympic Games. With one exception (the USA at Atlanta 1996) the host nation has always improved on its medal tally of four years earlier. That host country's medal tally four years later has fallen on each occasion."[8]

We sometimes give cheerleaders a bad rap today. But their role can be crucial, as in the case of a young man in our church who has begun to emerge as a striking leader. The Lord has used a number of things to awaken this sleeping giant from his napping youthful kingdom mediocrity, not the least of which has been his new wife. She enthusiastically believes in her husband. She discreetly communicates to him through her encouraging words and gestures her

7. D. L. Moody, *To the Work! To the Work!: Exhortations to Christians* (Chicago: P. H. Revell, 1884), chap. 3, http://archive.org/stream/toworktoworkexh00 moodgoog/toworktoworkexh00moodgoog_djvu.txt.

8. "Hosts with the Most: Why Home Advantage Brings More Olympic Medals," *Euronews.com*, July 28, 2016, https://www.euronews.com/2016/07/28/hosts-with-the -most-why-home-advantage-brings-more-olympic-medals.

conviction that he has been endowed as a highly gifted, mighty man of God. He believes her cheers, gets courage and energy from her, and continues to climb to unexpected heights. Incalculable are the blessings of a cheerleading wife. She echoes the apostle Paul, who gushes publicly about a young man in the Roman church: "Greet Rufus, chosen in the Lord" (Rom. 16:13).

4

Some Subtle Expressions of
ENCOURAGEMENT

The Lord grant mercy to the household of Onesiphorus, for
he often refreshed me, and was not ashamed of my chain.

—2 Timothy 1:16

King David gained access into Jebusite-inhabited Jerusalem not by
way of a direct, main gate, with a frontal assault, but instead indi-
rectly through a secret water tunnel (see 2 Sam. 5:6–9). Likewise,
we are wise to inject the adrenaline of encouragement not only
through the front door, using the direct methods we discussed in
the last chapter, but also by side-door, subtle, more indirect methods discussed in this chapter.

Physical Contact

At the end of Paul's greeting to the church at Rome, he urges the
saints to "greet one another with a holy kiss" (Rom. 16:16). A
kiss is a physical expression of love. This kind of kiss is a "holy"
(pure, consecrated, godly) kiss, as opposed to sensual, erotic, or
immoral. In the Judeo-Roman world of the first century, it was a
display of affection and support. Kissing another person's cheek,
forehead, beard, hands, and even feet was common. Such contact
was typically accompanied by an embrace that comprised warm
expressions of love and goodwill. The prodigal son's offended
father showers with kisses his returning-from-the-far-country boy:
"And he arose and came to his father. But when he was still a great

way off, his father saw him and had compassion, and ran and fell on his neck and kissed him" [literally, kissed him again and again] (Luke 15:20).

After Paul bids farewell to his dear Ephesian elder friends at Miletus, they kissed him: "Then they all wept freely, and fell on Paul's neck and kissed him, sorrowing most of all for the words which he spoke, that they would see his face no more. And they accompanied him to the ship" (Acts 20:37–38).

As we'll expand on later, this summons to display love by physical contact recognizes the importance of body language as an expression of encouragement to one another. Interpersonal touching is fundamental to human flourishing.

UCLA neuroscience researcher Alex Korb explains:

Holding hands with someone can help comfort you and your brain through painful situations. One fMRI study scanned married women as they were warned that they were about to get a small electric shock. While anticipating the painful shocks, the brain showed a predictable pattern of response in pain and worrying circuits.... During a separate scan, the women either held their husbands' hands or the hand of the experimenter. When a subject held her husband's hand, the threat of shock had a smaller effect. The brain showed…less activity in the pain and worrying circuits.[1]

James Merritt writes, "A simple touch can convey an incredible sense of love, affirmation, and acceptance. A study conducted at UCLA several years ago found that to maintain physical and emotional health, men and women need eight to ten meaningful touches each day. These researchers defined meaningful touch as a gentle tap, stroke, kiss, or hug, given by a 'significant other' such as a husband, wife, parent, or close friend."[2]

---

1. Eric Barker, "Neuroscience Reveals 4 Rituals That Will Make You Happy," *The Week*, February 28, 2016, http://theweek.com/articles/601157/neuroscience -reveals-4-rituals-that-make-happy.

2. As quoted in Maxwell, *Encouragement Changes Everything*, 77.

I'll never forget the day my dad died. At seventy-one, he had been the picture of good health. When I arrived at the hospital, there lay my best counselor friend in the whole world and my life hero. He was on an emergency room gurney, and when I smothered him in an embrace, he was cold and clammy. He'd been such a good dad! But he was gone. That day I understood the trauma of David's fighting men, who "lifted up their voices and wept, until they had no more power to weep" (1 Sam. 30:4). My wife was in Europe that week with her sister and didn't know anything yet. I was alone.

That evening, when Wednesday prayer meeting was starting, I was drained and exhausted, and I didn't want to go. But I felt I had to go to be with my friends, my family, in my Father's house. Late, I slipped into the back row of the auditorium and heard brothers praying about the loss of Dad. I sat silently sobbing. Jennifer, a wise woman and mother, saw me out of the corner of her eye and came back and buried me briefly in a holy embrace. That timely embrace, that sisterly touch, that "holy kiss" was such medicine to my wounded heart. It ministered more to my parched soul than the river of words that washed over me that whole week. Encouraging physical contact is important.

For many years, I ran the 25 kilometer (15.5 miles) River Bank Run road race in my hometown of Grand Rapids, Michigan. But for the past few years, I've run only the early morning 5k race. Upon finishing, after I cool down I've made it a habit to drive across town to John Ball Park where the 25k runners are only about 2.5 miles from their finish line, chiefly to encourage friends who are trying to complete their body-and-soul-testing marathons. I clap my hands, shout out emboldening "attaboys," telling exhausted, ashen-faced, about-to-faint runners that they can do it, that they are almost there, and that they are amazing to have already made it so far in such a short time. I shout these things because I remember how empowering it was when bystanders said such things to ready-to-quit me over the years.

It is interesting how many total strangers hear and see me on the curb and veer over to my side of the road, reach out their hand, and just want to touch me with a high five. It seems like it gives them an adrenaline surge. Most of my friends want more than a high five. They want a hug.

As we are all running the marathon race of life, each of us should study how we can encourage one another by enlisting the "holy kiss" principle of physical contact at strategic locations along the route.

Saying Thank You

Paul is purposeful and careful to direct words of thanks to those (Priscilla, Aquila, the Gentile churches) who have risked much and spent much to assist him in his kingdom exploits: "Greet Priscilla and Aquila, my fellow workers in Christ Jesus, who risked their own necks for my life, to whom not only I give thanks, but also all the churches of the Gentiles" (Rom. 16:3–4). Elsewhere he writes to the church at Philippi regarding their generous financial support: "Indeed I have all and abound. I am full, having received from Epaphroditus the things sent from you, a sweet-smelling aroma, an acceptable sacrifice, well pleasing to God. And my God shall supply all your need according to His riches in glory by Christ Jesus" (Phil. 4:18–19).

William Stidger was pastor of a church during the Great Depression, a time when people often bemoaned their hardships, provoking each other into personal depression and even suicidal thoughts. Stidger resolved instead to be thankful—to God and to people. The first person to pop into his mind was his high school English teacher, whose love of literature inspired him to become a pastor. That night he sat down and wrote a simple letter of thanks to her. Within a few days he received back a feebly scrawled note:

My Dear Willy,

I can't tell you how much your note meant to me. I am in my eighties, living alone in a small room, cooking my own meals, lonely, like the last leaf of autumn lingering behind.

You'll be interested to know that I taught in school for more than fifty years, and yours is the first note of appreciation I have ever received. It came on a blue, cold morning, and it cheered me as nothing has done in many years.

This heartwarming response brought an emotional bull market to Stidger's soul, motivating him to try again. He thought of an old, retired bishop whose wife had passed away in recent months. The bishop had given helpful counsel to Stidger when he was a young pastor. Stidger mailed another note. A couple of days later a return note came:

Your letter was so beautiful, so real, that as I sat reading it in my study, tears fell from my eyes, tears of gratitude. Before I realized what I was doing, I rose from my chair and called my wife's name to share it with her, forgetting she was gone.

You'll never know how much your letter has warmed my spirit. I have been walking around in the glow of your letter all day long.[3]

Last year I was fearing and trembling while working through, seeking to update, and breathing new life into some old notes on my biblical interpretation (hermeneutics) lectures. I had to teach a concentrated module on that theme in a seminary. It was a daunting twenty hours of classroom lectures in four days. I felt overwhelmed and discouraged, scrounging through what seemed like stale material that smelled like spoiled manna. But then, out of the blue, I received this two-decade-late thank-you note from an old friend who knew of my upcoming task: "About twenty years ago or more, we went through your hermeneutics videos in a leadership group

---

3. Nancy DeMoss Wolgemuth and Lawrence Kimbrough, *Choosing Gratitude: Your Journey to Joy* (Chicago: Moody, 2009), 120–21.

at our church…. Don't presume on grace. I believe you won't. But just go through your old notes, and they will bless the hearers as they did us way back then!" What a rush that timely "thank you" gave me! God used it. It gave me a surge of in-the-study inspiration, and the dreaded week went splendidly.

I've heard and read of pastors who keep a special file of notes, cards, and letters from people over the years who have taken the time to express their thanks to them. The gospel ministry can be a great blessing, but it can also be soul-withering. In seasons of fainting, these men will occasionally dip into the thank-you file and be reinvigorated by adrenaline shots of personal gratitude. I must confess that I have a priceless file of my own. Thank you, dear friends, for taking the time to brighten my eyes.

Body Language

On this subject, we venture beyond Paul's encouragements to the church at Rome. According to Albert Mehrabian's oft-quoted study on verbal and nonverbal messages, our words account for only 7 percent of our communication, while tone of voice accounts for 38 percent, and body language accounts for 55 percent.[4] This indicates that some of our most influential and effective interacting is done without words.

Cain's bitter attitude toward God was eloquently expressed in his face: he "was very angry, and his countenance [face] fell" (Gen. 4:5). The Lord understood that Cain's body language effectively communicated his sour heart. He said to Cain, "Why are you angry? And why has your countenance fallen?" (v. 6).

After years of brotherly feuding, Jacob and Esau communicated volumes to each other without a word at their reunion. Jacob "bowed himself to the ground seven times, until he came near to his brother. But Esau ran to meet him, and embraced him, and fell on his neck and kissed him, and they wept" (Gen. 33:3–4).

---

4. Albert Mehrabian, *Silent Messages: Implicit Communication of Emotions and Attitudes,* 2nd ed. (Belmont, Calif.: Wadsworth, 1981).

Yes, outward body language gestures communicate much—for healing or for hurting:

> A worthless person, a wicked man…
> winks with his eyes,
> He shuffles [signals with] his feet,
> He points with his fingers;
> Perversity is in his heart,
> He devises evil continually,
> He sows discord. (Prov. 6:12–14)

Our Lord Jesus silently delivered a world of hurt to Peter's triple-denying soul by just expressively and disappointingly locking eyes with him: "And the Lord turned and looked at Peter" (Luke 22:61). Distraught, Peter "went out and wept bitterly" (v. 62).

Eutychus conveyed a lack of interest in Paul's late-night Troas sermon by "sinking into a deep sleep" (Acts 20:9). The fire of a pastor's sermon can be damagingly doused by a drowsy listener or powerfully fueled by an animated hearer. Attentive eyes, an occasional nod, a timely smile, and an alert leaning forward in the pew can encourage a preacher into delivering the truth with peculiar power. That is right. A congregation can in many ways make or break a sermon.

Queen Esther was anxiously unsure of King Ahasuerus's heart toward her as she stood uninvited in the royal hall within eyeshot of his throne. Would he summon her in or sentence her to death? The king said not a word, but "held out to Esther the golden scepter that was in his hand. Then Esther came near and touched the top of the scepter" (Est. 5:2). She was encouraged by Ahasuerus's body language!

Humor and Irony

As mentioned earlier, sometimes the finest-wine forms of encouragement aren't the overt and obvious. The subtle and refined versions may be the best. Creative irony and clever humor can be wonderfully therapeutic. Consider the following verses:

A merry heart does good, like medicine,
But a broken spirit dries the bones. (Prov. 17:22)

A time to weep,
And a time to laugh;
A time to mourn,
And a time to dance. (Eccl. 3:4)

A. W. Tozer wrote, "Few things are as useful in the Christian life as a gentle sense of humor."[5]

Many decades ago in London, "a young Member of Parliament, when making his maiden speech in the House of Commons, was overcome by intense nervousness. Gradually, his shyness in addressing the House vanished, and he said what he had to say and sat down. Then his nervousness returned and he felt that he had blundered. Miserable, a note was passed to him with only two words, 'You'll do.' They were initialed by the greatest Statesman of the day. The Member kept those kind and clever words as a treasured souvenir and a perpetual encouragement."[6]

George W. Bush therapeutically used humor in eulogizing Senator John McCain at his dignitary-packed 2018 funeral in the National Cathedral: "Cindy and the McCain Family, I am honored to be with you to offer my sympathies and to celebrate a great life.... Some lives are so vivid, it's difficult to imagine them ended. Some voices are so vibrant and distinctive, it is difficult to think of them stilled. A man who seldom rested is laid to rest, and his absence is tangible, like the silence after a mighty roar.... I'll miss him. Moments before my last debate ever, with Senator John Kerry in Phoenix, I was trying to gather some thoughts in the holding room. I felt a presence, opened my eyes, and six inches from my face was McCain, who yelled: 'Relax! Relax!'" An immediate roar

---

5. A. W. Tozer, "The Use and Abuse of Humor," *Alliance Weekly*, November 14, 1951.

6. A Naismith, *2,400 Scripture Outlines, Anecdotes, Notes, and Quotes* (Grand Rapids: Baker, 1973).

of affectionate laughter filled the cathedral, warming and encouraging the hearts of the grieving McCains.[7]

Humor has a wonderful way of healingly maneuvering into otherwise hard-to-access places.

Presence

Just showing up and being there can mean more than a world of words. David benefited from the mere presence of Jonathan: "So David saw that Saul had come out to seek his life. And David was in the Wilderness of Ziph in a forest. Then Jonathan, Saul's son, arose and went to David in the woods and strengthened his hand in God" (1 Sam. 23:15–16).

Job benefited from the mere presence of his three friends: "Now when Job's three friends heard of all this adversity that had come upon him, each one came from his own place—Eliphaz the Temanite, Bildad the Shuhite, and Zophar the Naamathite. For they had made an appointment together to come and mourn with him, and to comfort him.... They sat down with him on the ground seven days and seven nights, and no one spoke a word to him, for they saw that his grief was very great" (Job 2:11–13). Their presence was medicine. The problems began when they opened their mouths.

Our Lord craved the mere presence of His three best friends: "Then Jesus came with them to a place called Gethsemane, and said to the disciples, 'Sit here while I go and pray over there.' And He took with Him Peter and the two sons of Zebedee, and He began to be sorrowful and deeply distressed. Then He said to them, 'My soul is exceedingly sorrowful, even to death. Stay here and watch with Me'" (Matt. 26:36–38).

Onesiphorus was there for Paul when it counted: "The Lord grant mercy to the household of Onesiphorus, for he often

---

7. George W. Bush, eulogy for John McCain, *PBS News Hour Weekend*, September 1 2018, https://www.pbs.org/newshour/politics/watch-george-w-bushs-full -eulogy-for-john-mccain.

refreshed me, and was not ashamed of my chain; but when he arrived in Rome, he sought me out very zealously and found me" (2 Tim. 1:16–17).

Back in January 1988 my wife and I had moved away from our family for me to serve as pastor at a church near Dayton, Ohio. When the six-month ultrasound disclosed that the little boy Dianne was carrying had a serious birth defect, spina bifida, we were devastated. When my dad and mom heard about it, they immediately drove down from Michigan through the snow. I don't remember much of what they said, but I'll never forget the price-less balm of their presence. They were there. They stood with us and strengthened us.

We were down and troubled, and we needed a helping hand. They came running to see us again. All we had to do was call. Yes, it was winter, but it could have been spring, summer, or fall. They were just there, as a friend.

Empathy

Sometimes you feel like a failure and are certain that no respect-able person would ever be in an embarrassing situation like the one you are in. The week after graduating from seminary, I spent most of my time packing up my young family's possessions into a rental truck so we could move to Dayton, Ohio, to take up my first pastorate. But before I could leave on Monday, I had to preach at my home church on Sunday morning. A Saturday night thun-derstorm had left the church building without electrical power. I began the sermon preaching by candlelight. This added to the stress I already felt about my lack of preparation during the week. About fifteen minutes into my message, things weren't going well. I began to perspire. Darkness crept in from the corners of my vision. And I blacked out and collapsed on the platform! My wife thought maybe she had been left a widow with two little boys. But thankfully a couple of men leaped onto the stage and revived me. Someone shouted that an ambulance should be called. I protested, returned to the pulpit, apologized for my excessive nervousness, confessed that it was my sinful pride that created my panic, and finished my sermon.

That afternoon, I was sitting at home, so embarrassed, wondering if I would become known as the "fainting pastor" who couldn't handle the ministry due to a black-out phobia. The phone rang. It was a man who had been a pastor for many years. "Hey, Mark, don't worry about it. That same thing happened to me once. The Lord got me through it. In fact there's an interesting chapter in Charles Spurgeon's book *Lectures to My Students* titled 'The Minister's Fainting Fits.' You might find it helpful."

That is empathy. It is encouraging another person by letting him or her know that you've experienced the same thing yourself, by putting yourself in his or her shoes. And for me, the Lord used it as a shot of adrenaline.

The Scriptures are full of encouraging empathy:

No temptation has overtaken you except such as is common to man; but God is faithful, who will not allow you to be tempted beyond what you are able, but with the temptation will also make the way of escape, that you may be able to bear it. (1 Cor. 10:13)

Blessed be the God and Father of our Lord Jesus Christ, the Father of mercies and God of all comfort, who comforts us in all our tribulation, that we may be able to comfort those who are in any trouble, with the comfort with which we ourselves are comforted by God....

For we do not want you to be ignorant, brethren, of our trouble which came to us in Asia: that we were burdened beyond measure, above strength, so that we despaired even of life. Yes, we had the sentence of death in ourselves, that we should not trust in ourselves but in God who raises the dead. (2 Cor. 1:3–4, 8–9)

Falling into sin and denying Christ by morally traitorous behavior has laid low many a child of God. We become so ashamed and wonder if we can ever be restored again to the joy of our salvation (Ps. 51:12) or ever be used by God to serve His kingdom. Peter's empathy revives us. He is the one who provided the apostolic eyewitness accounts for the Gospel of Mark. It is generally recognized that John Mark was Peter's penman—that Peter told Mark what to write. And Mark's Gospel doesn't spare Peter regarding his triple denial of our Lord, but even more than the other Gospels tells all. That is the way Peter wanted it:

> Now as Peter was below in the courtyard, one of the servant girls of the high priest came. And when she saw Peter warming himself, she looked at him and said, "You also were with Jesus of Nazareth."
>
> But he denied it, saying, "I neither know nor understand what you are saying." And he went out on the porch, and a rooster crowed.
>
> And the servant girl saw him again, and began to say to those who stood by, "This is one of them." But he denied it again.
>
> And a little later those who stood by said to Peter again, "Surely you are one of them; for you are a Galilean, and your speech shows it."
>
> Then he began to curse and swear, "I do not know this Man of whom you speak!"
>
> A second time the rooster crowed. Then Peter called to mind the word that Jesus had said to him, "Before the rooster crows twice, you will deny Me three times." And when he thought about it, he wept. (Mark 14:66–72)

Peter's empathy says to us, "Ashamed brothers and sisters, look at me! I failed miserably—not just once or twice—but three times. I collapsed in the face of servant girls and a maid. I punctuated my denial with cursing and swearing. But the Lord Jesus is so gracious that He restored even the likes of me to a crucial place of leadership in His church" (see Mark 16:7; John 21:15–22).

John Mark probably entered the empathy parade himself by cryptically telling his own shameful story of cowardly collapse: "Now a certain young man followed Him, having a linen cloth thrown around his naked body. And the young men laid hold of him, and he left the linen cloth and fled from them naked" (Mark 14:51–52).

This is probably the young John Mark's not-so-secret confession of his first embarrassing failure of abandoning the Lord in Gethsemane.[8] And it wouldn't be his last failure. Remember that Mark cowardly quit a mission, leaving Paul and Barnabas alone in the mountains of Pamphylia and returning to his mother in Jerusalem during Paul's first journey (Acts 13:13). But eventually the Lord restored even this shameful "quitter" to usefulness, not only to Peter as the penman of the first Gospel (according to Mark) but also to Paul as a fellow missionary: "Only Luke is with me. Get Mark and bring him with you, for he is useful to me for ministry" (2 Tim. 4:11). That really encourages failures like me!

Henry Cloud tells of an embarrassing business mistake he made that resulted in his company's hemorrhaging dollars at a dangerous rate. Then the phone rang. This was before caller ID. A voice asked him what was going on.

> It was my main business mentor at that time, one of the most influential people in my life.
>
> My heart sank…. I was ashamed of where I was and ashamed that I was going to have to admit it all to him….
>
> "I have really screwed up," I confessed. I proceeded to tell him the entire story. I had blown it. Really blown it.
>
> He was silent on the other end of the line. I was waiting for him to just rip into me and scold me for what I had done. And then he said it: "Well, we've all been there."
>
> Wait…what did he say? I thought, Did he say "we"? As in, him too? "Who? Been where?" I asked.

---

8. Lane, *Gospel According to Mark*, 527.

"We've all made that mistake," he said. "We've all hired the wrong person or done a deal with the wrong partner, when we should have seen it coming. And paid dearly for it."...

As we continued talking, as he understood and cared, something happened in me. Something huge.... It was like some light breaking through in a dark storm. What had happened?... Nothing about the situation had changed. Except one thing: I had tapped into the power of the other. After our talk, I now had energy and the courage to get to work. My tank was full.[9]

9. Henry Cloud, *The Power of the Other: The Startling Effect Other People Have on You, from the Boardroom to the Bedroom and Beyond—and What to Do about It* (New York: Harper Business, 2016), 72–74.

5

The Gospel as the Ultimate
ENCOURAGEMENT

> *'Tis music in the sinner's ears,*
> *'Tis life and health and peace.*
> —Charles Wesley

This truth that giving encouragement is an adrenaline shot for the soul isn't just a camouflaged version of today's prevalent Moralistic Therapeutic Deism (MTD). MTD is a term coined by sociologists Christian Smith and Melinda Lundquist Denton in their 2005 book *Soul Searching: The Religious and Spiritual Lives of American Teenagers.* MTD is exposed as a subtle new theology that has been smuggled into Christian circles. It craftily presents God as a cosmic therapist who coaches people to enjoy successful living through happiness, self-esteem, and fulfilling relationships. It teaches people that the central goal of life is to be happy and to feel good about themselves.

An epitomizing meme depicts the god of MTD. Out of an Aladdin's lamp swirls an at-your-service genie butler. His hair is well combed. His bow tie is perfectly straight. A napkin is draped over his poised forearm. He says, "Hello there. You rang? How can I make you feel better right now? How can I serve you? Wow, you're looking nice today! You are just the greatest thing ever, aren't you? I am so lucky to be your god!"

That is not what this book is about. That is not what all these numerous scriptural quotations are saying. On the contrary, the "adrenaline for the soul" emphasis in this book is biblically based

encouragement medicine prescribed for sinners from the perspective that the gospel of salvation in Jesus Christ alone imparts
the eternal life every soul needs to avert the eternal depression of
outer darkness in hell. Only justification by faith and regeneration
by God's Spirit can bring true joy and enduring peace. Any self-
help treatment short of this spiritual new birth is tragically and
fatally nearsighted.

The Gospel Saves for Eternity

Around the middle of the nineteenth century, Moritz Retzsch
painted a masterpiece titled *Checkmate*. It is a gripping scene with
a piece-filled chessboard as its centerpiece. On one side of the
board is the devil, and on the other side is a young man. The devil
has the expression of a triumphant predator about to close in for
the kill. The youth looks like a stunned and hopeless victim, cor-
nered with no way of escape. Tears are welling up in his eyes. He
has been checkmated, and there is no way out. It depicts the moral
tragedy of life when naïve youths sell their souls to Satan and sur-
render to him in utter despair.

Legend has it that this painting hung in a prominent place
where a group of men were admiring its creative brilliance. One
member of the group was an accomplished chess master who was
transfixed by the configuration of the pieces on the board. When
the others walked away, he kept staring. After a time, he shouted
out, "There is a move! It's not checkmate! There is a move!"[1]

The truth is we've all sold our souls to Satan and sit tragically
checkmated by our sinful treachery against God. I recently met a
twenty-six-year-old young man, Nate, who came to carpet our living room. He was listening to Christian music on his phone, and
my wife asked him about his faith. Out from him flowed a striking
testimony of how the Lord looked on a pathetic marine who had

---

1. "Anecdote of Morphy," *Columbia Chess Chronicle* 3, no. 7, 8 (August 18, 1888):
60, One-More-Move-Chess-Art.com, https://www.one-more-move-chess-art.com
/One-More-Move.html.

sinned in unmentionable ways in Afghanistan, resulting in a broken life, a collapsing marriage, and a pair of endangered children. He had been licked by Satan, was haunted by his sinful record, and was wallowing in depression, just waiting for the shoe of eternal punishment to drop for his high moral crimes against God. He was hopelessly whipped. But then someone gave him the gospel. There was one move he could make! He could go to Christ. And he did.

The gospel is the ultimate word of encouragement to fainting and collapsing souls. There is a move! You can go to Jesus Christ. He can rescue, save, and snatch you from your death-row bench.

The checkmated marine Nate, any criminal hell-deserving sinner, and I can go to the cross of Christ. You can go to Him right now. Come with me to an ugly skull-shaped hill outside Jerusalem back in AD 30. There Jesus hung naked, nailed to the cross. The Bible records His loud cry at the ninth hour: "'Eli, Eli, lama sabachthani?' that is, 'My God, My God, why have You forsaken Me?'" (Matt. 27:46). What's going on here?

Jesus is taking the "electric chair" of eternal punishment for six long hours in the place of sinners. He has been banished to the hellish horror of teeth-gnashing outer darkness, away from the smile and favor of His Father. He is undergoing God's wrath that sinners deserve. He is taking our hell. He is sacrificing Himself as our substitute. All the sins of His criminal friends at that moment in time were legally imputed to Jesus, borne by Him in the depths of His infinite soul.

> Oh, to see the pain,
> Written on Your face,
> Bearing the awesome weight of sin;
> Ev'ry bitter thought,
> Ev'ry evil deed,
> Crowning Your bloodstained brow.
> This, the pow'r of the cross:
> Christ became sin for us;

Took the blame, bore the wrath—
We stand forgiven at the cross.[2]

Spurgeon once preached regarding Christ's cry of dereliction from the cross, "This voice out of 'the belly of hell' marks the lowest depth of the Saviour's grief. The desertion was real."[3] He continued,

> We believe this agony was equal to the agonies of the lost in hell.... And remember, not the equivalent for the agony of one, but an equivalent for the hells of all that innumerable host of souls whose sins He bore, condensed into one black cup to be drained in a few hours. The miseries of an eternity without an end, miseries caused by a God infinitely angry because of an awful rebellion, and these miseries multiplied by the millions for whom the man Jesus Christ stood as covenant head. What a bitter cup that was.... And yet he drained that cup, drained it down to its last dregs. Not a drop was left.[4]

Having drained that bitter cup, Jesus shouted in triumph, "'It is finished!' And bowing His head, He gave up His spirit" (John 19:30; see also Matt. 27:50). Spurgeon gives the ultimate encouragement to his own previously checkmated, guilty soul: "For you, my soul, no flames of hell; for Christ the Paschal Lamb has been roasted in that fire. For you, my soul, no torments of the damned, for Christ has been condemned in your place."[5]

Jesus's great work on the cross for sinners accomplished what our good works never could. It is a futile move for us to rely on our good works. They are rubbish. Go to Jesus and believe only in His

---

2. "The Power of the Cross," Words and Music by Keith Getty and Stuart Townend, © 2005 ThankYou Music (PRS), adm. worldwide at CapitolCMGPublishing.com excluding Europe which is adm. by IntegrityMusic.com.

3. C. H. Spurgeon, sermon 2133, in *The Metropolitan Tabernacle Pulpit: Sermons* (Passmore & Alabaster, 1856), 134.

4. C. H. Spurgeon, "Christ Perfect through Sufferings (sermon 478)," *Metropolitan Tabernacle Pulpit*, vol. 8, November 2, 1862, Spurgeon Center for Biblical Preaching at Midwestern Seminary, http://www.spurgeon.org/resource-library /sermons/christ-perfect-through-sufferings.

5. Spurgeon, "Christ Perfect through Sufferings."

finished work on the cross for sinners, "knowing that a man is not justified by the works of the law but by faith in Jesus Christ.... We have believed in Christ Jesus, that we might be justified by faith in Christ and not by the works of the law; for by the works of the law no flesh shall be justified" (Gal. 2:16).

It is the simple gospel: "For God so loved the world that He gave His only begotten Son, that whoever believes in Him should not perish but have everlasting life" (John 3:16).

In December 2016, I was at the bedside of a dear Christian brother, Glenn, who was dying of cancer. He was almost skeletal. At the time I was visiting him, he was told he probably had only a couple weeks to live. Sometimes in the dark of night Glenn would get discouraged and afraid. Then his sins would rise up as roaring dragons, and his assurance of being heaven-bound was shaken. He showed me a piece of paper on which he had scratched Romans 10:9: "If you confess with your mouth the Lord Jesus and believe in your heart that God has raised Him from the dead, you will be saved." He told me that this promise was his only hope. I did the best I could to encourage him to cling to that gospel promise as a drowning man clings to a life preserver in a stormy sea: "Be encouraged, Glenn! Christ will hold you fast!"

When Glenn's cancer storm ended and he washed up on the shore of another world, I'm thinking he was greeted by angels who escorted him into the presence of the Judge of all the earth. There Glenn stood. There the devil might have appeared, accusing Glenn of all his recorded crimes of thought, word, and deed: "Surely this filthy sinner is mine. He has sold his soul to me. He has sinned away any right to be Yours. He is guilty of high crimes against Your law. He is a criminal deserving forever punishment in hell." That is when Glenn opened his hand, uncrumpled his scrap of paper, and boldly read it aloud, confessing Jesus as his Lord and Savior who died on the cross and rose for him. It was like reciting the song that Glenn and I frequently rehearsed together: "Just as I am without one plea, but that Thy blood was shed for me."

And I'm thinking Jesus then strode forward, showed His wounded hands and feet, and declared that He has already taken Glenn's sentence, hung in Glenn's place, was strapped in Glenn's "electric chair" while on the cross, took the full voltage of His Father's wrath for Glenn's sins, and paid in full Glenn's infinite debt to God's justice. Then I'm thinking Glenn got a change of clothing. The filthy rags of Glenn's sinful performance were exchanged for the radiant white linen of Christ's perfect obedience. And dressed like that, Glenn was escorted past an annoyed Satan, past the stairway leading down to hell, and into the most excellent of all banquets celebrating the homecoming of Jesus's blood-bought friends.

Here is a prophetic sketch of the drama I think occurs for Glenn and all who sincerely believe the gospel after they go to heaven. Here, the high priest represents God's sinful people. He stands as a condemned prisoner in the dock:

> Then he showed me Joshua the high priest standing before the Angel of the LORD, and Satan standing at his right hand to oppose him. And the LORD said to Satan, "The LORD rebuke you, Satan! The LORD who has chosen Jerusalem rebuke you! Is this not a brand plucked from the fire?"
>
> Now Joshua was clothed with filthy garments, and was standing before the Angel.
>
> Then He answered and spoke to those who stood before Him, saying, "Take away the filthy garments from him." And to him He said, "See, I have removed your iniquity from you, and I will clothe you with rich robes."
>
> And I said, "Let them put a clean turban on his head."
>
> So they put a clean turban on his head, and they put the clothes on him. And the Angel of the LORD stood by. (Zech. 3:1–5)

The Gospel Provides Acceptance with God

We need to understand that this gospel encouragement isn't only for the dying. It is also for the living—in every conceivable circumstance. For example, it is for women who desperately want to be supermoms but find they can't measure up. In her book *Christ in the Chaos: How the Gospel Changes Motherhood*, Kimm Crandall tells of her spiritual odyssey as a mother. She got pregnant and was immediately deluged by her Christian women friends and mentors with books and pamphlets telling her how much to eat, how precisely to exercise, exactly how much weight to gain, how to train for labor, breastfeed, and manage diapers. She writes, "I was going to be a quiverfull, all-natural, homeschooling, dress-wearing, bread-baking, whole-foods-eating mother. Then the babies came. And came and came and came. That was it. I couldn't be the kind of mother I wanted to be—the kind of woman I honestly regarded as more godly than others. So I labeled myself a failure and spent the next several years in a terrible depression. Yes, years."[6]

It all came to a head one evening as she sat in the dark, rocking in a chair, reflecting how miserably she had fallen short that day, having impatiently scolded her son, cursed aloud within earshot of her daughter, and neglected the needs of her husband. She sat convicted in her guilt cell. Her motherhood odyssey had led her to despair of herself, feeling like she had fallen so far short. She couldn't do this—be the got-it-altogether supermom God deserved her to be. She thought that God could never love her, but instead would kick her away in disgust. It was time for her to run afresh to the cross to be reminded of the only way to find acceptance with God.

Kimm needed a shot of the adrenaline truth of the gospel. In mommy meltdown moments, Christian women don't need to fundamentally be reminded of the "what-would-Jesus-do" behavior list, but of the "what-Jesus-already-did" gospel balm. Kimm put it this way: "Jesus is not only my example…. He's my replacement. He came to do everything I haven't done and could never do, and He did it sinlessly and perfectly."[7] Jesus never had a moral meltdown and never lashed out in profanity at His disciples or enemies, even

---

6. Kimm Crandall, *Christ in the Chaos: How the Gospel Changes Motherhood* (Adelphi, Md.: Cruciform Press, 2013), 26.

7. Crandall, *Christ in the Chaos*, 58.

when heads were wagging at Him on the cross. On the cross, Jesus wore Kimm's humiliating dunce cap so that in her rocking chair she might wear His impressive crown of righteousness. And wearing the apparel of Christ's righteousness, Kimm sits accepted in the lap of her heavenly Father, in whose eyes Kimm is as adored as His perfectly obedient Son, of whom He said, "This is my beloved Son, in whom I am well pleased." In Christ alone, a shamed mommy finds herself affectionately loved by God.

Elyse Fitzpatrick helps failures rocking in dark rooms by commenting, "It's [Jesus's] delight to dress you in garments that befit your calling as the bride of the Lord of lords." She then quotes Isaiah 61:10:

> I will greatly rejoice in the LORD,
> My soul shall be joyful in my God;
> For He has clothed me with the garments of salvation,
> He has covered me with the robe of righteousness,
> As a bridegroom decks himself with ornaments,
> And as a bride adorns herself with her jewels.

She continues:

> He has clothed you in "a robe of righteousness."... When he looks at you, he smiles with contentment and deep affection.... You are radiant, without any stain or shadow of guilt...glistening, white, pure....
>
> Then, when we focus too narrowly on our sin,... we're like a bride who insanely shreds her gown...and then hides in a corner, ashamed, self-condemning, wretched. All she sees is her shame....
>
> This is what [Christ] thinks when he looks upon his bride: *Isn't she magnificent! She's gorgeous, glorious, noble, honorable.* And remember this: you're not beautiful just because you have been allowed to play dress-up with some other beautiful bride's wardrobe; no, he's made *you* holy—spirit, soul, and body.... We're not playing dress-up. This is who we really are.[8]

---

8. Elyse Fitzpatrick, *Comforts from the Cross: Celebrating the Gospel One Day at a Time* (Wheaton, Ill.: Crossway, 2011), 23–25.

Could it really be that though we deserve God's repulsed disgust, in Christ we instead get God's well-pleased affirmation, His enthusiastic commendation, and His delighted praise? That is the wonder of the gospel! In Christ we please and delight Him. He even rejoices over us with singing (Zeph. 3:17). The apostle Paul points this out throughout his epistles:

> For he is not a Jew who is one outwardly, nor is circumcision that which is outward in the flesh; but he is a Jew who is one inwardly; and circumcision is that of the heart, in the Spirit, not in the letter; whose praise is not from men but from God. (Rom. 2:28–29)

> But "he who glories [boasts, NASB], let him glory [boast] in the LORD." For not he who commends himself is approved, but whom the Lord commends. (2 Cor. 10:17–18)

As creatures made in the image of God, we instinctively pine and ache for affirmation and praise! Tim Keller drives it home to our insecure yet pining hearts this way:

> All your life you've been knocking on a door, "Affirm me! Love me! Tell me I'm okay!" You've been…working all of your relationships so that somehow you can steal self-acceptance from other people. It never works. But in the gospel, the door at which you've been knocking will open at last.…
>
> And now, finally, the only pair of Eyes in the universe whose opinion counts…looks at you and sees an absolute beauty! Finally the door on which you've been knocking all your life has been opened at last. And now the natural world ceases to have any claim on you! Who cares what they think now! Now criticism doesn't kill you![9]

---

9. Tim Keller, "Boasting in Nothing Except the Cross," session 9, 2017 TGC National Conference, Indianapolis, Ind., April 5, 2017, The Gospel Coalition Resource Library, http://resources.thegospelcoalition.org/library/boasting-in -nothing-except-the-cross.

The gospel is the ultimate word of affirming encouragement to our knocking, trembling, aching, insecure souls. This kind of perfect love casts out all fear of people—and of anything else!

The Gospel Is an Antidote for Worry

For many people worry is a corrosive and common companion. Arthur Somers Roche writes, "Worry is a thin stream of fear trickling through the mind. If encouraged, it cuts a channel into which all other thoughts are drained." Michel de Montaigne observes, "My life has been filled with terrible misfortune; most of which never happened."[10]

Worry whispers despair-producing lies into the ears of God's safe and secure children. Worry seeks to make atheists of theists, telling us that our sovereign Father isn't even there. Worry tells us we are defenseless orphans hurtling aimlessly through time and the universe with absolutely no one caring for our concerns. Like Chicken Little crying out that the sky is falling, worry chirps that at any moment we could chaotically crash into a chance calamity, causing a crushing and catastrophic collapse. Lies!

The gospel tells us otherwise. Our heavenly Father has foreknown us since before the foundation of the world. He is actively causing all things to work for our good. He predestined us to our adoption as sons and daughters. He spared not His own Son, but freely gave Him up for us all. That almighty, risen, and ascended Son ever lives and intercedes for us. No one or thing can separate us from the love of Christ. He will never leave us or forsake us.

When Christ was on the cross, all the powers of hell were unleashed on Him. He was destitute of a doting Father's care. Loaded down with the foul sins of the world, Jesus saw the fatherly back turned away from Him, leaving Him outside in the frigid cold, suffering an excruciating lack of peace. This was a crushing, catastrophic collapse.

---

10. As quoted in Natalie H. Ragland, *Encourage Yourself in the Lord* (Bloomington, Ind.: Westbow Press, 2018), 226.

Ending up crashed in such a God-forsaken heap is a disaster worth worrying about. But for the child of God, such a crash is a theological impossibility. The gospel says, "Because the Son of God was forsaken, the child of God will never be forsaken." Because He was abandoned to darkest blackness, the child of God never will be. The gospel says, "I will never leave you nor forsake you" (Heb. 13:5). Child of God, nothing can separate you "from the love of God which is in Christ Jesus our Lord" (Rom. 8:39).

The best antidote to worry, fretting, and despairing is telling ourselves the truth with the encouragement of the gospel. Yes, we need to encourage ourselves by talking to ourselves about the grace of God. Prone-to-worry-and-depression David frequently encourages himself this way in the Psalms. Psalm 42:11 is only one example:

> Why are you cast down, O my soul?
> And why are you disquieted within me?
> *Hope in God*;
> For I shall yet praise Him,
> The help of my countenance and my God.

D. Martyn Lloyd-Jones writes in his book *Spiritual Depression*:

> Have you realized that most of your unhappiness in life is due to the fact that you are listening to yourself instead of talking to yourself? Take those thoughts that come to you the moment you wake up in the morning. You have not originated them, but they start talking to you, they bring back the problems of yesterday, etc. Somebody is talking. Now David's treatment was this; instead of allowing this self to talk to him, he starts talking to himself. "Why art thou cast down, O my soul?" he asks. His soul had been depressing him, crushing him. So he stands up and says: "Self, listen for a moment, I will speak to you."[11]

Encourage yourself with the gospel.

---

11. D. Martyn Lloyd-Jones, *Spiritual Depression: Its Causes and Cure* (Grand Rapids: Eerdmans, 2005), 20–21.

The Gospel Is a Cure-All for Every Spiritual Ailment

In Greek mythology, Panacea was the goddess of the universal remedy. She is actually mentioned at the opening of the earliest version of the Hippocratic Oath taken by physicians. Legend has it that she possessed a potion that was a cure-all for any physical malady. So whether a child was fevered, a warrior wounded, or a king diseased, Panacea could say, "Pour the potion into that." The gospel is a lot like that. It is a real cure-all for every discouraging life malady. Pour the gospel into that!

John Stott views the gospel in this way: "All progress in the Christian life depends upon a recapitulation of the original terms of one's acceptance with God."[12] Stott here directs us to the time-less remedy for all our ailments, including spiritual depression and beyond. In the Christian life, we never outgrow the need to daily and even hourly remind ourselves of the gospel. Every step we take on the spiritual battlefield in facing foes such as disappoint-ment, anger, bitterness, resentment, hopelessness, temptation, fear, selfishness, and weakness requires us to deliberately revisit and remind ourselves of the gospel. Pour the gospel into that!

Late in the apostle Paul's life, he was surrounded by a host of discouraging circumstances. He was imprisoned in Rome, soon to be executed. Heresies abounded in the churches. Treachery and defections had invaded even his inner circle of companions. Nearly all his friends had abandoned him. All these things were against him. But he writes to Timothy, encouraging himself and his protégé with the gospel truth that God is able and does wonder-fully turn the tables from despair to delight. "Remember that Jesus Christ, of the seed of David, was raised from the dead according to my gospel, for which I suffer trouble as an evildoer, even to the point of chains; but the word of God is not chained" (2 Tim. 2:8–9). B. B. Warfield concludes, "To Paul, it is clear, the resurrection of

---

12. John R. W. Stott, *The Cross of Christ*, 20th anniversary ed. (Downers Grove, Ill.: IVP Books, 2006), 27.

Christ was the hinge on which turned all his hopes and all his confidence, in life and also in death."[13]

That first Lord's Day morning, when the tomb was sealed shut, harboring a dead body, everything was gloomy and depressing. But in an instant, with a supernatural burst of resurrection power, God graciously turned the tables. He changed mourning and weeping into rejoicing and dancing. That is the gospel hope and encouragement we feed on in our darkest hours. Take heart, Christian! The Lord Jesus is able to resurrect your joy in an instant.

Jesus is not dead. He is risen and ascended and has gathered into His sovereign hands the reins of the universe. He is Lord of all. He is supernaturally causing all things to work for your good. Warfield comments, "If our hearts should fail us as we stand over against the hosts of wickedness which surround us, let us encourage ourselves and one another with the great reminder: Remember Jesus Christ, risen from the dead, of the seed of David!"[14] That is the gospel.

A church has taken a severe blow and is down and discouraged. The risen Lord Jesus is able to supernaturally raise it back up by just speaking a word. A young lady is devastated due to a romantic breakup. A middle-aged man in his midfifties has been fired and vocationally left for dead. A depressed woman is so discouraged and spiritually lifeless she can't get out of bed.

Dear fainting children of God, remember Jesus Christ, risen from the dead, according to Paul's gospel. It is spiritual adrenaline. Trust Him who is able to soon make you dance: "Weeping may endure for a night, but joy comes in the morning" (Ps. 30:5).

A retired Christian man was battling severe back pain. Without forewarning, lightning-like strikes pierced his spine, sending him reeling in agony. He was so thankful for the pain relief that Vicodin provided. But then he came to the sobering realization

---

13. B. B. Warfield, "The Risen Jesus," Monergism, accessed May 29, 2018, https://www.monergism.com/risen-jesus.

14. Warfield, "The Risen Jesus."

that he was trapped in an addiction to this gripping opioid. Needing to ween himself off this pain reliever, he found himself battling depression. Horrible addiction is on the right. Unbearable affliction is on the left. The enemy is whispering, "Curse God and die." He is whimpering, "It would be better if I'd never been born! Surely, God has abandoned me!" Pour the gospel into that!

Brother, there is an inheritance reserved in heaven for you, one that is incorruptible, undefiled, and won't fade away (1 Peter 1:4). "For our light affliction, which is but for a moment, is working for us a far more exceeding and eternal weight of glory" (2 Cor. 4:17). If God spared not His own Son to save you and so is clearly for you, who can be against you? How will He not give you whatever you need in this dilemma (Rom. 8:31–32)? God has not abandoned you. To the contrary, the entire Trinity is unitedly conspiring for you. The Son is standing at the right hand of the Father interceding for you. The Spirit is mightily stirring and striving within you. The Father is sovereignly causing all things to work for your good.

I know a man who participated in sexual perversion in his youth and is haunted with feelings of indelible moral filthiness. I know another man who cheated on his wife, and though she forgave him, he is still plagued with paralyzing guilt. I know still another man who has visited internet whorehouses where he has looked at women, committing adultery of the heart. And I know a man who recklessly miscalculated while driving his truck and crashed into a motorist, resulting in the death of someone's precious son. I know a man who, due to his own folly, committed a serious business blunder, causing the bankrupting of his business and the collapsing of his large family's comfortable standard of living. All these men battle with bouts of strangling dejection. Pour the gospel into that!

On the cross Jesus has taken these matters into His own hands, holding the list of charges against you, absorbing in His palm the hammered-in spikes, and wonderfully removing your guilt and shame. Jesus Christ, "having wiped out the handwriting of requirements that was against us, which was contrary to us...has taken it out of the way, having nailed it to the cross" (Col. 2:14).

Jared Wilson helps guilty men who sit in rocking chairs: "I think every man carries around some sort of wound, baggage, things that they've done, mistakes that they've made, sins that they've committed. Even if they've repented of these things, sometimes they don't feel forgiven or they feel like they can't escape from under that shadow. The gospel comes in and says that what you've done does not define you. You are what God says you are in Christ. Understanding the rich truth of justification gives us great freedom from the past."[15]

A young man was drowning in a besetting sin. Between swallows at the coffee shop, he told me it is an addiction he fears he just can't break. He expressed that surely no genuine Christian would ever have this spiritual battle going on inside of him, that surely he is hopelessly lost! We opened the Bible to Romans 7, where Paul gives an autobiographical account of his own battle as a Christian:

> For the good that I will to do, I do not do; but the evil I will not to do, that I practice. Now if I do what I will not to do, it is no longer I who do it, but sin that dwells in me.
>
> I find then a law, that evil is present with me, the one who wills to do good. For I delight in the law of God according to the inward man. But I see another law in my members, warring against the law of my mind, and bringing me into captivity to the law of sin which is in my members. O wretched man that I am! Who will deliver me from this body of death? I thank God—through Jesus Christ our Lord! (Rom. 7:19–25)

Be encouraged! You are not the only real Christian engaged in intense spiritual warfare! And in that battle, you have to fight fire with fire—pleasure with pleasure! That smartphone screen promises you a big swallow of pleasure if you just tap on it and indulge in forbidden fruit. But the Bible promises you a far greater pleasure

---

15. Jared Wilson, "3 Ways the Gospel Encourages Weary Men," November 25, 2015, Articles, Crossway, https://www.crossway.org/articles/3-ways-the-gospel-encourages-weary-men/.

if you pocket the phone and walk away. That swallow may be sweet in the mouth for a moment but will surely be nauseatingly sour in the belly of your conscience for a long time. Basking in the smile and nearness of God with a clean conscience is a far sweeter and enduring pleasure: "In Your presence is fullness of joy; at Your right hand are pleasures forevermore" (Ps. 16:11). Be encouraged by and employ that available and wonderful gospel maneuver of killing the deceitful pleasures of sin with the superior pleasures of Christ. Pour the gospel into that.

And also my tempted brother, be encouraged with your true spiritual identity in Christ—who you really are as a born-again Christian. You are not an old man and slave to sin anymore. You are a new man, more than a conqueror in Christ (Rom. 6:11–18; Eph. 4:22–24). Don't go back to the vomit of that sin. You are better than that! You are not a lap dog of Satan anymore. You are a mighty man-child of God Almighty! I'm not flattering you. But I am pumping you up with truths more potent than adrenaline. I'm telling you like it is! Be encouraged by who you really are in Christ, and act like it!

We never outgrow our need for the gospel. It is a cure-all panacea to our dying day. One Saturday morning in early January 2017, my brother Glenn finished his uphill marathon against cancer. A few nights earlier, I read to him from Malachi 4:2 describing a sinner's final-day liberation:

> But to you who fear My name
> The Sun of Righteousness shall arise
> With healing in His wings;
> And you shall go out
> And grow fat like stall-fed calves.

Other Bible translations say that those calves go out of the barn leaping and frolicking. I asked Glenn, who had been a dairy farmer for years, "What's that all about?" His ashen face lit up: "When a calf has been pent up all winter in a barn stall, in the spring you swing open the barn door, they run and jump all around like crazy!"

I tried to encourage him: "That is you, Glenn! You're all pent up in this skeletal body pinned to this old hospice bed. But it won't be long, and the barn door will be thrown open, and you'll be set free into paradise like a calf released from a stall. You're almost there!" Within a little over a week, right there on that farm, skeletal Glenn breathed his last and experienced reality.

Gospel encouragement is the most potent adrenaline of all. We should tell it to others, and we should tell it to ourselves.

The Gospel Is for You

Maybe you are reading this book, suffocating in hopelessness, having sold your soul to the devil by overdosing way too many times on forbidden fruit. I'm right there with you. Checkmated. Sentenced. Doomed. But there is a move! You can go to Jesus! The hymn writer Charles Wesley captured this well:

> Jesus! the name that charms our fears,
> That bids our sorrows cease;
> 'Tis music in the sinner's ears,
> 'Tis life and health and peace.

Jesus will rescue, save, and snatch you from your death-row bench. "Believe on the Lord Jesus Christ, and you will be saved" (Acts 16:31). By God's freely offered grace, any criminal, hell-deserving sinner can go to the cross of Christ. Put the book down, right now, and go to Him.

6

The Personal Disinclinations to
ENCOURAGEMENT

I had not noticed how the humblest, and at the same time most balanced and capacious minds praise most, while the cranks, misfits, and malcontents praised least.

—C. S. Lewis

Giving encouragement really does provide an adrenaline shot for the soul. So if it is true that encouragement brings to those around us such beneficial exhilaration, fulfills before God such scriptural obligation, and finds so many avenues for daily expression, why are most of us so lacking in our encouraging?

David Murray insightfully summarizes, "Praising others does not come easily to human nature; we like to receive praise, but not to give it. Criticizing comes much easier because we feel more comfortable looking down on people. Praising involves looking up in admiration, and our necks and egos tend to creak and ache when we attempt it. Affirmation is also discouraged by powerful societal trends: cynicism, distrust, suspicion, negativity, envy, political strife, and bad news at home and abroad, all combine to chill our hearts and shrink our souls."[1]

Recently, I visited a couple who had moved into a condominium complex that featured a pond, the outdoor centerpiece of a nicely landscaped park. Left to itself, that pond water would become stagnant and naturally scum over with a foul algae film

---

1. Murray, "Practicing Affirmation."

and aroma. But the owner of the complex had wisely installed a beautiful fountain in the middle of the pond. It bubbled up sparkling sprays, splashed delightful droplets, stirred up the still surface, aerated the lively waters, and serenaded the whole park scene. Everybody wants a unit with a view of the pond from their back deck.

Our mouths should be fountains that bubble up with encouragement. But too often we are more like still ponds, and those around us don't enjoy the benefit of the sparkling influence we could have. Why? A host of things can disincline us to being Barnabas-like encouragers; in this chapter we will look at hindrances within ourselves that choke off the free flow.

Our Egotistical Jealousy

We are all born with self as the default idol of the soul. We natively crave to be king of the mountain and ascend to a status of superiority above our neighbors. Praise God that saving grace can put to death our self-idolatry, and through the Spirit we can esteem others more highly than ourselves by truly loving our neighbors.

But often that crucified old man, in the form of indwelling sin, tries to claw its way out of the grave. The "flesh lusts against the Spirit" (Gal. 5:17). And self-idolatry in the form of egotistical jealousy can subconsciously reside in our hearts with great effectiveness, keeping us from speaking encouraging words to others. That is why we may find it more natural to cut down others with our words than to build them up.

If we can put a person down a rung or two on the social status ladder, that will naturally bump us up a rung or two. That may be what we subconsciously crave. That may be why we have the propensity to put down and the aversion to lift up. It is easy to be unmotivated to encourage.

Sandy sits next to Pamela in the auditorium during the high school orchestra concert. Pamela's daughter plays first violin and flawlessly completes a beautiful solo. Sandy's daughter is the second violinist, who sat still and silent during the solo. Sandy aches for her disappointed daughter, who, weeks earlier, lost the competition for first violin. That is what makes it so difficult for Sandy to pat Pamela on the shoulder and encouragingly congratulate her on her daughter's magnificent performance. Yet for Sandy to do so is to humble herself and show love to Pamela in spite of her personal disappointment, demonstrating the truth of a saying by an unknown author, "It takes more grace than I can tell, to play the second fiddle well."

One competitive father confessed openly to our Sunday school class, "I find the obligation to 'rejoice with those who rejoice' (Rom. 12:15), one of the most difficult to meet in the whole Bible." Your brother's son gets a scholarship when your son doesn't. It is hard to give resounding congratulations.

King Saul's son Jonathan, who was next in line to become king, saw David courageously step up in the valley of Elah and slay the giant Goliath. He saw the undeniable power of God resting on this youthful rival who had, in effect, stepped in line ahead of him when he was anointed to become the next king of Israel. What did Jonathan do? He encouraged David: "Then Jonathan and David made a covenant, because he [Jonathan] loved him as his own soul. And Jonathan took off the robe that was on him and gave it to David, with his armor, even to his sword and his bow and his belt" (1 Sam. 18:3–4). That is gracious. Well done, Jonathan! His fleshly instinct may have been to silently pout in disappointment. Instead, he praised with encouragement.

What a thrill it is to view Tim joining the evening youth group and see his cousin Phil across the room. They are both varsity high school soccer players. Voting took place last week for All-Conference honors. Phil was chosen. Tim wasn't. But Tim, realizing nobody has yet heard the news and probably never will unless he says something, shouts across the crowded room, "Hey everybody, let's hear it for my cousin Phil who got All Conference! He's a beast of a midfielder." That is gracious. Well done, Tim!

Our Pleading for Integrity

A father might ask, "But if my son has the ability to achieve all As on his report card, why would I ever commend and encourage him when he gets mostly Bs?" And a wife might question, "If my husband needs to lose fifty pounds, why would I compliment him when he has lost only ten?"

These critical questions are basically pleas for integrity. We want to be honest and not pretend. We can be disinclined to encourage for what we may view as an inferior performance because we don't want the recipient of our praise to believe an illusion. We might think that we need to be truthful and that it is ungodly to applaud for less than excellence.

We would do well to consider what godliness really is. It is godly to imitate God. And the God of heaven, who holds the highest of excellence standards, is a great encourager! He encourages His people continuously though we disappointingly underperform continuously.

Consider Job. God did. God knew that Job was a sinner whose life was riddled with moral blemishes and iniquities. Job himself confessed his awareness of God's knowledge of his troublesome sins that could be dumped out into a courtroom to haunt him: "My transgression is sealed up in a bag, and You cover my iniquity" (Job 14:17).

One reason for Job's personal trial was the Lord's fatherly chastising and refining him for his own good: "Man is also chastened with pain on his bed" (Job 33:19). "But He knows the way that I take; when He has tested me, I shall come forth as gold" (23:10). Job's indwelling sin problem needed purging: "Therefore I abhor myself, and I repent in dust and ashes" (42:6).

No one thoroughly knew Job's poor underperformance like the Lord did. Under the Lord's holy gaze, Job was shamefully deficient. Nevertheless, notice the encouraging praise and boasting the Lord heaps on Job in the heavenly courts: "Then the LORD said to Satan, 'Have you considered My servant Job, that there is none like him on the earth, a blameless and upright man, one who fears God and shuns evil?'" (Job 1:8). Look at that and take note. Stumbling and faltering Job gets high praise from God Most High!

Notice also the way that the master in the parable of the talents heaps praise and commendation on the performance of his laboring servants:

> After a long time the lord of those servants came and settled accounts with them.
>
> So he who had received five talents came and brought five other talents, saying, "Lord, you delivered to me five talents; look, I have gained five more talents besides them." His lord said to him, "*Well done,* good and faithful servant; you were faithful over a few things, I will make you ruler over many things. Enter into the joy of your lord." He also who had received two talents came and said, "Lord, you delivered to me two talents; look, I have gained two more talents besides them." His lord said to him, "*Well done,* good and faithful servant; you have been faithful over a few things, I will make you ruler over many things. Enter into the joy of your lord." (Matt. 25:19–23)

The parable's earthly master is a picture of our heavenly Father, who is clearly not stingy, but generous in pouring out encouraging commendation on His still stumbling, bumbling, underperforming servants. If God displays Himself as magnanimous and generous in pouring out praise, how dare we be stingy and miserly in refusing to give out "Well dones!" to those who live in our orbit?

The Duke of Wellington, the British military leader who defeated Napoleon at Waterloo, was not an easy man to serve under. He was brilliant and demanding, and not one to shower his subordinates with compliments. Yet even Wellington realized that his methods left something to be desired. Winston Churchill once reported of a reply made by the Duke of Wellington, in his last years, when a friend asked him: "If you had your life over again, is there any way in which you could have done better?" The old Duke replied: "Yes, I should have given more praise."[2]

Our Dislike of Dale Carnegie

In 1936, Dale Carnegie wrote a best-selling self-help book titled *How to Win Friends and Influence People*. To date, it has sold almost thirty million copies. It is viewed by many Christians as a bad book—a manual for cultivating unhealthy techniques of social manipulation. As a result, many Christians instinctively shrink back from anything that even remotely resembles the social behavior recommended by Carnegie—forms of encouragement such as being careful to mention someone's name, commending a job well done, or publicizing a private act of nobility.

The book does have some bad things in it. Carnegie goes too far in manipulatively contriving and promoting interpersonal strategies for gaining friends. In February 2015 on his *Thinking in Public* podcast, Albert Mohler interviewed historian Steven Watts, author of *Self-Help Messiah: Dale Carnegie and Success in Modern America*. Mohler perceptively traced elements of Carnegie's theology of self-help from Phineas Quimby, to Norman Vincent Peale, to Robert Schuler, to Joel Osteen, to Oprah Winfrey. Carnegie's folly was skillfully exposed.

But Mohler also divulged elements of undeniable good that are to be found in Carnegie's classic book. He admitted that the book causes a bit of a divide in him because he had been so helped by it when he read it as a fifteen-year-old who had a lot to learn about "how to respond to someone, how to keep a conversation going, how to shake a hand, how to understand the importance of an individual's name. All of these things really are important. They're kind of what my grandfather called consecrated common sense." At the same time, Mohler admits that "this is a horrifying book… filled with heresy."

---

2. Mark Adkin, *The Waterloo Companion* (Mechanicsburg, Pa.: Stackpole Books, 2001), 131.

Watts echoed Mohler's willingness to acknowledge great good in Carnegie: "I'd also add that…at least for portions of that book, the advice is kind of a variation of the golden rule—you know, treating other people the way you would like to be treated, respecting other people, and giving other people their due, and giving other people room to express themselves. Up to a certain point, I think the book is fine. There's even a kind of innocence to it. It's very attractive in that way."[3]

All this is to say that we should not stumble at the biblical concept of encouragement simply because it was championed by a man like Dale Carnegie, who took it and ran with it to an extreme. Just because Dale Carnegie champions a truth doesn't make it an untruth. Carnegie profoundly and helpfully wrote, "You have it easily in your power to increase the sum total of this world's happiness now. How? By giving a few words of sincere appreciation to someone who is lonely or discouraged. Perhaps you will forget tomorrow the kind words you say today, but the recipient may cherish them over a lifetime."[4]

We should always remember the apostle Paul's instruction to the church at Thessalonica: "Test all things; hold fast what is good. Abstain from every form of evil" (1 Thess. 5:21–22). It is true that Carnegie has in some ways given encouragement a bad name and has abused the virtue. But simply because something is abusable doesn't mean it is disposable. So it is with encouragement.

Our Default Setting of Cranky Criticism

David Murray has confessed, "I'm a Scot, and Scots don't do praise. Of God sometimes, but we never praise one another. Instead, we specialize in pulling people down, thinking the worst of others, and

---

3. Albert Mohler, "Self-Help in Modern America: A Conversation with Historian Steven Watts," *Thinking in Public*, AlbertMohler.com, February 16, 2015, https://albertmohler.com/2015/02/16/thinking-in-public-watts/.

4. Dale Carnegie, *The Quick and Easy Way to Effective Speaking* (Uttar Pradesh, India: Om Books, 2017), 153.

puncturing anyone who achieves anything. We can't let a compliment pass without balancing it with criticism, and we betide [cut down to size] people who make anything of their lives: 'They're just full of themselves.'"[5]

My wife often told me of a tired, old, burned-out librarian who worked downtown at the local branch. She seemed to thrive by critically nitpicking on the patrons. "Quiet! You're being too loud.... You do realize that this whole bag of books is being returned four days late.... I know you're a regular here, but if you forgot your card, you can't take home any books!... Don't lean on the counter.... The children shouldn't be playing on the stairs."

But at the same library, on a different day, there may be a refreshing, motivated, encouraging librarian who transforms the overcast bleak weather into sparkling sunshine. "Your children are so happy!... Don't worry about being a couple of days late with those books; you're usually so conscientious.... No card? No problem! You're one of our favorite customers!... I love the way you read to your kids with such expression." Though it is the same library, it is a transformed climate and experience.

Some people seem to get a strange sense of satisfaction in displaying a superior upper hand over others, and they use disapproving words and body language to assert their dominance. They can't afford to appreciate and encourage because they've hardwired themselves to criticize and belittle. They've become cranky and ornery. All of us have found ourselves at least occasionally slipping into this ditch.

The hawk's eye for flaws and the bat's eye for virtues betray a kind of soul sickness that fails to recognize the teeming things praiseworthy in others made in the image of God. C. S. Lewis wrote, "The world rings with praise—lovers praising their beloveds, readers their favorite poet, walkers praising the countryside, players praising their favorite game—praise of weather, wines, dishes, actors, motors, horses, colleges, countries, historical personages,

---

5. Murray, *Happy Christian*, 121.

children, flowers, mountains, rare stamps, rare beetles, even sometimes politicians or scholars. I had not noticed how the humblest, and at the same time most balanced and capacious minds praise most, while the cranks, misfits, and malcontents praised least."[6]

Jude gives no quarter to a murmuring, ornery disposition when he describes the self-obsessed false prophets of his day: "These are grumblers, complainers [finding fault, NASB], walking according to their own lusts" (Jude 16).

In commenting on Hebrews 10:24—"Consider one another in order to stir up love and good works"—Spurgeon warns against a cantankerous, hypercritical spirit:

> I am afraid there are some who consider one another to provoke in quite a different spirit from this—who watch to find out a tender spot where a wound will be most felt. They observe the weakness of a brother's constitution, and then play on it, or make jests about it. All this is evil, so let us avoid it; let us all seek out for the good points of our brethren, and consider them, that we may afterwards be the means of guiding them to those peculiar good deeds for which they are best adapted.[7]

A cranky, critical spirit isn't merely a personality quirk. It is a spiritual problem that calls for putting it off in repentance and putting on its contrasting virtue—an encouraging, praising spirit.

Our Self-Preoccupation

Simply put, we are often too obsessed and consumed with our own personal struggles to dispense encouragement to others. Or, as John Piper puts it more pointedly, "When our mouths are empty of

---

6. C. S. Lewis, *Reflections on the Psalms* (San Francisco: HarperCollins, 2017), 94–95.

7. C. H. Spurgeon, "Spurgeon's Verse Expositions of the Bible (Hebrews 10)," StudyLight.org, accessed May 29, 2018, https://www.studylight.org/commentaries /spe/hebrews-10.html.

praise for others, it is probably because our hearts are full of love for self."[8]

I can remember my freshman year of college. I came from a high school where I knew almost everybody and almost everybody knew me. But now things were different. All I saw on campus were unfamiliar faces that looked right through me instead of recognizable faces warmly greeting me. I'd wake up early in the morning, in the dark, and didn't want to climb out of bed, get dressed, and head off to class. The sparkle was gone. No one knew my name. I was lonely and isolated.

During the summer prior to my senior year in high school, the Lord wonderfully saved me at a Fellowship of Christian Athletes camp. And one of the evidences of the new birth in me was the Spirit's stirring me to come out of my self-fixation and look on others with kind consideration, sometimes expressed through loving words of encouragement. But as a freshman in college, my encouragement fountain had been stopped up by my self-obsessed loneliness. I was in a brotherly love backslide. I became so fixated on my own emotional swamp that I lost my ability to perceive others in the hallway who were going under and were in need of a smile or the adrenaline shot of a word of encouragement in the classroom or library. I was too focused on me to have an eye for others. By the Spirit, I needed to repent of that, as should all believers who are so self-pitying that they can't be an encouragement to others.

After the church service, we need to turn our eyes away from ourselves and look around. It is a mission field. We are there to serve others. We should desire first to give help to others and not to seek esteem from associating with popular people who make us feel significant. Like the Lord Jesus, we should esteem others more highly than ourselves by dispensing encouraging words, even when we are swamped ourselves.

---

8. John Piper, foreword to *Practicing Affirmation: God-Centered Praise of Those Who Are Not God*, by Sam Crabtree (Wheaton, Ill.: Crossway, 2011), 7, http://public .eblib.com/choice/publicfullrecord.aspx?p=1059441.

Think of our Lord Jesus. He was drowning on Golgotha in the deep waters of His horror on the cross. But even there, His head was still up, looking out for and tending to the needs of others, dispensing strategic shots of neighbor-targeted kindness. To his deeply sorrowing mother, He encouragingly spoke, "Woman, behold your son," addressing her widow housing needs. Regarding his persecuting enemies, He encouragingly spoke, "Father, forgive them, for they know not what they do," addressing their spiritual and eternal needs. To the distressed thief at his side, he encouragingly spoke, "This day you will be with Me in paradise," fueling his faith needs. Even on the cross, our Lord wasn't self-obsessed and blind to the fainting condition of others. He gave the timely shot of encouragement adrenaline.

7

The Social Disinclinations to
ENCOURAGEMENT

The mouth of the righteous is a fountain of life.
—Proverbs 10:11 ESV

Our mouths should be fountains that bubble up with enlivening encouragement. As discussed in the last chapter, we must clear away our personal heart issues that disincline us and clog up a godly, Spirit-filled flow. But our disinclinations to praising others are not only exclusively inward and personal in nature but also outward and social. We may actually fear that our encouraging others will have detrimental effects—on them! Let's explore in this chapter those social disinclinations that would choke off free-flowing expressions of encouragement.

Our Fear of Stagnation

We can refrain from encouraging because we fear that approval given prematurely may result in a stagnated performance before a desired goal is achieved. A father stares at the report card of his son, who hasn't been performing academically up to his potential. This card is better than the last few, which have averaged 5 Cs and 1 D. This one records 4 Bs and 2 Cs. But the father believes his son has the potential to earn 4 As and 2 Bs. Dad feels reluctant to encourage his son at this point because he fears his son will stagnate and be satisfied with this underachieving performance level. Can you feel the reluctance?

A 1994 letter to *Reader's Digest* depicts the true effect of encouragement: "One morning I opened the door to get the newspaper and was surprised to see a strange little dog with our paper in his mouth. Delighted with this unexpected 'delivery service,' I fed him some treats. The following morning I was horrified to see the same dog sitting in front of our door wagging his tail, surrounded by eight newspapers. I spent the rest of the morning returning the papers to their owners."[1]

Let's revisit the man who should lose fifty pounds. He has lost ten pounds, but all his wife can see is the forty that still need to go. So she is reluctant to say, "Looking good!" I mentioned Proverbs 12:25 earlier: "Anxiety in the heart of man causes depression [literally, weighs it down], but a good word makes it glad." A good word of encouragement makes a weighed-down man glad, and if he is working hard to lose weight, he'll feel light as a feather when his wife compliments him on his progress. I contend that congratulating him robustly for losing ten pounds is the best way to spur him on to dropping forty more.

Furthermore, building a relationship is like maintaining a bank account. You have to make periodic deposits in order to eventually make beneficial withdrawals. Pointing out positives and strengths in other people can display that we are on their side and incline them to take our advice to heart when we have some constructive criticism down the road. So in the long run, generous encouragement tactfully produces momentum and acceleration, not stagnation.

David Murray says it well: "Far from discouraging change, encouraging the less than perfect actually maximizes the chances of their continuing to progress. Just recall who helped you learn at school or make progress in sports. They were the teachers and coaches who praised and encouraged you, weren't they? Praise opens our ears and pushes us through the pain barrier."[2]

---

1. Marion Gilbert, in *Reader's Digest* 144, no. 862 (February 1994): 12.

2. David P. Murray, *The Happy Christian: Ten Ways to Be a Joyful Believer in a Gloomy World* (Nashville: Nelson, 2015), 128.

Our Contempt for Flattery

In November 2015, John Piper was asked, "How do I praise others but avoid flattery?" He wisely warned about the real danger of encouraging praise deteriorating into sinful flattery:

> The Greek word for flattery…occurs one time in the New Testament. Paul is defending his ministry to the Thessalonians and he says, "We never came with flattering speech as you know, nor with a pretext for greed, nor did we seek glory from men either from you or from others" (1 Thessalonians 2:5–6). And it is, I think, more than coincidental that flattery occurs in that sentence with the word *greed*.
>
> In other words, I want something from you. You can kind of get at the heart of flattery when you think about that.…
>
> Now lots more is said about flattery in the Old Testament than in the New Testament. The word *flatter* is built on the Hebrew word for "to be smooth or slippery."… The most general statement about flattery, in its destructive effects, is Proverbs 26:28: "A flattering mouth works ruin." Or Proverbs 29:5: "A man who flatters his neighbor is spreading a net for his steps."[3]

But Piper is also earnest in stressing the importance of encouraging, affirming, and praising others in whose lives we see God's good handiwork. He calls the absence of affirming encouragement a kind of sacrilege—for at least three reasons:

> First, it is disobedience to God's command: "A woman who fears the Lord is to be praised" (Prov. 31:30). And I can't think of any reason why this does not apply in the principle of God-fearing men.
>
> Second, it demeans Jesus as though he were stooping to do something unworthy when he says, "Well done, good and

---

3. John Piper, "How Do I Praise Others but Avoid Flattery?," *Ask Pastor John*, Desiring God, November 2, 2015, https://www.desiringgod.org/interviews/how-do-i-praise-others-but-avoid-flattery.

faithful servant" (Matt. 25:21, 23). If he says it, should we consider it beneath us to say it?

Third, all the works of God are worthy of praise. And
there is no good in anyone but by the work of God (1 Cor.
4:7: 15:10).[4]

So again we see that simply because something can be abused
doesn't mean it is disposable. Giving can deteriorate into bribery,
but keep giving—carefully! Getting can deteriorate into greed, but
keep getting—carefully! Encouraging can deteriorate into flattery,
but keep encouraging—carefully!

Yes, beware. The blessing of encouragement and praise can
become excessive, as Proverbs reminds us.

> Have you found honey?
> Eat only as much as you need,
> Lest you be filled with it and vomit. (25:16)

So don't exaggerate. Praise proportionately. Give bronze praise for
bronze accomplishments, silver for silver, and gold for gold. Don't
overdo it.

Before we leave the flattery theme, consider this: it is sinful to
be chronically suspicious of the motives of others. If you find yourself habitually ascribing negative designs to those who praise you,
it is best to conclude that the problem is not theirs, but yours. It is
best to seek to repent of your unloving treatment of the people who
are encouraging you. Love…"believes all things" (1 Cor. 13:7). Love
thinks the best of others. It doesn't regularly accuse of ill motives.

Our Concern about Pampering People

An old tree in our yard died of Dutch elm disease, so I cut it down
with "T-I-M-B-E-R!" drama for the amusement of our grandson
Richard. The excitement over, it was time to cut the tree apart limb
from limb and drag the branches to the burn pile. But after one

---

4. Piper, foreword to *Practicing Affirmation*, 8.

trip, Richard was tired of it and wasn't interested in cooperating anymore. For me to have encouraged him by saying, "Great job, Richard!" would have been like giving his team a trophy for a T-ball baseball season record of 1 win and 9 losses. That kind of disingenuous self-esteem pampering is counterproductive. The problem of pampering students into fragile helplessness is well documented.

In an *Education World* article titled "Can Adults Praise Children Too Much?" Ellen R. Delisio explains:

> Identifying a child's strengths and developing those strengths helps build confidence more than constant praise does.... Praise also loses its effect if the praise is the same for all the students. For example, if all the students in a class are told their paintings are great and students know some are better than others, the praise will lose its significance.... Adults have gotten into the habit of not telling children when they are wrong, and that will not help them cope with adversity when they are adults in the real world....
>
> Although the idea that praise for children should be more selective and specific is not new, it is starting to overtake the notion that more praise always is better, according to Benjamin Mardel, a researcher with Harvard University's Project Zero.... Mardel also commented that he would not want to see the pendulum swing back to the other extreme where teachers withhold praise for genuine accomplishments. "The joy and excitement of learning can co-exist with some of the tension and anxiety that's also part of learning," he said.[5]

Reporting for ABC News, Liz Neporent discusses the findings of a Dutch study that warns of the adverse effects of excessive praise:

> Make your kid believe he's a "special snowflake" and you risk turning him into a narcissistic jerk, according to a new Dutch study.... That's because over-praising children can lead them to believe they are special people who deserve special

---

5. Ellen R. Delisio, "Can Adults Praise Children Too Much?," *Education World*, accessed May 29, 2018, http://www.educationworld.com/a_curr/curr302.shtml.

treatment all the time, explained Brad Bushman, a professor of communication and psychology at Ohio State University and one of the study's authors.

"Parents should be warm and loving, but not give their child blanket praise," Bushman said. "We should not boost self-esteem and hope our children will behave well. Instead, we should praise our children after they do well."[6]

Biblical wisdom regarding moderation helps here: "It is not good to eat much honey" (Prov. 25:27). It is also good not to overdose in giving too much praise.

Our Aversion to Feeding an Affirmation Addiction

A good friend of mine who is a business executive once confided in me, "I'm an affirmation junkie!" He was saying that he loves the high he gets from people telling him when he does a good job. But he also dislikes that he feels empty and unappreciated when praise doesn't come. He confessed that this love of encouragement tempts him at times to make decisions calculated to court the approval of men instead of the approval of God.

That tension is a common one. What motivates me, as a pastor preparing sermons, when it is time to choose applications from a Bible passage? I can think, "How will this one play in the lobby after the worship service? Will folks commend me or condemn me for it? Will they verbally admire me or ignore me?"

Robert P. George gave good advice to young Christian scholars on the dangers of seeking affirmation:

> Although it is natural and, in itself, good to desire and even seek affirmation, do not fall in love with applause. It is a drug. When you get some of it, you crave more. It can easily deflect you from your mission and vocation. In the end, what matters is not winning approval or gaining celebrity. Your

---

6. Liz Neporent, "Too Much Praise Can Turn Your Kids into Narcissistic Jerks, Study Finds," *ABC News*, March 9, 2015, https://abcnews.go.com/Health/praise-turn-kids-narcissistic-jerks-study-finds/story?id=29506856.

mission and vocation is to seek the truth and to speak the truth as God gives you to grasp it…. We are all vulnerable to the drug. The vulnerability never completely disappears. And the drug is toxic to the activity of thinking (and thus to the cause of truth-seeking).[7]

This is an important spiritual wrestling mat for all Christians: "The fear of man brings a snare" (Prov. 29:25). And a fundamental mark of godliness is a soul so circumcised by the Spirit that his "praise is not from men but from God" (Rom. 2:29). Wrestle we must. But clearly the solution is not to discredit and dispense with affirmation and praise.

Years ago, I was part of an ordination service for a fledgling pastor. The guest preacher warned the young man's new congregation about how vulnerable he would be to their compliments and expressions of appreciation: "Be careful not to bring a snare to him by commending his sermons." The dear preacher meant well, but I wanted to stand up and shout out a balancing exhortation: "Don't let this young man starve from a lack of encouraging and appreciative feedback to his sermons!" I fear that a large contributor to pastoral burnout in many good men is a severe shortage of wise, Barnabas-borne "well dones." Spurgeon wrote:

> You remember the story of the man who had a good wife, and one said to him, "Why, she is worth her weight in gold."
>
> "Yes," he said, "she is worth a Gibraltar rock in gold, but I never tell her that. You know that it is necessary to maintain discipline, and, if I were to tell her how much I really value her, she would not know herself."
>
> Well, now, that is wrong. It does people good to be told how highly we value them. There is many a Christian man and woman, who would do better if now and then someone

7. Robert P. George, "Advice to Young Scholars," *First Things*, August 2, 2014, https://www.firstthings.com/blogs/firstthoughts/2014/08/advice-to-young-scholars.

would speak a kindly word to them, and let them know they had done well.[8]

Again, give and eat honey, but don't overdo it, lest you make others sick and they vomit.

Our Reluctance to Scratch the Human Pride Itch

Arguably the greatest track race of all time took place at the 1954 Commonwealth Games in Vancouver. To this day it is still called the "miracle mile." For almost four laps Roger Bannister ran hard at the heels of the first-place runner, John Landy, at a world record sub-four-minute pace. Then it happened. Landy glanced back to his left, and Bannister blasted by to his right, taking the lead and the win.

God's glory is to have the first place in our souls, but it seems that human pride is ever running hard at God's heels to gain that position of preeminence. So in this fierce, lifelong spiritual competition for preeminence, why would we want to give an adrenaline shot to human pride by encouraging, cheering on, or in any way applauding a person? By heartily affirming people, aren't we just scratching their insatiable itch for self-exaltation? These are healthy questions.

C. S. Lewis warns, "As long as we have the itch of self regard, we shall want the pleasure of self approval; but the happiest moments are those when we forget our precious selves and have neither."[9]

John Piper warns, "Our fatal error is believing that wanting to be happy means wanting to be made much of. It feels so good to

8. Charles H. Spurgeon, "Both Sides of the Shield," *Spurgeon's Sermons*, vol. 37, no. 613, ed. Larry and Marion Pierce for Answers in Genesis, "Spurgeon Sermons," June 6, 2017, https://answersingenesis.org/education/spurgeon-sermons/2233-both-sides-of-the-shield/.

9. C. S. Lewis and Walter Hooper, *The Collected Letters of C. S. Lewis* (San Francisco: HarperSanFrancisco, 2004), 3:429.

be affirmed. But the good feeling is finally rooted in the worth of self, not the worth of God. This path to happiness is an illusion."[10]

The Lord warns in Jeremiah 9:23:

> Let not the wise man glory in his wisdom,
> Let not the mighty man glory in his might,
> Nor let the rich man glory in his riches.

The Lord also cautions, "The crucible is for silver and the furnace for gold, and each is tested by the praise accorded him" (Prov. 27:21 NASB). Derek Kidner comments, "The proportions of praise meted out to Saul and David in 1 Samuel 18:7 ('Saul has slain his thousands, and David his ten thousands.') threw both men into the crucible."[11] John reports regarding the hardhearted Pharisees: "They loved the praise of men more than the praise of God" (John 12:43).

We must always remember the biblical doctrine of the sinfulness of humanity. But we misapply that doctrine if it drives us to muzzle our appreciation of humanity, and especially redeemed humanity. We've already seen that C. S. Lewis, John Piper, and supremely the Lord Himself have all strongly endorsed praising and encouraging one another. Just because medicine can be converted into poison doesn't mean it ceases to be medicine when properly administered and ingested.

John Bunyan was once told that he had just done well in preaching a good sermon, and his reply was, "The devil already told me that as I was coming down the pulpit stairs."[12] Any preacher with a conscience says amen to that anecdote. But there is a healthy tension that we should maintain, and this anecdote from Martyn Lloyd-Jones gives a corrective tug in the encouragement direction. In his book originally titled *Don't Wait Till He's Dead! Everybody Needs Encouragement Now!*, Derick Bingham recounts

---

10. John Piper, *God Is the Gospel: Meditations on God's Love as the Gift of Himself* (Wheaton, Ill.: Crossway, 2005), 13.

11. Kidner, *Proverbs*, 168.

12. William Barclay, *The Gospel of Matthew* (Edinburgh: Saint Andrew Press, 1965), 2:102.

how the renowned preacher Lloyd-Jones was once told that his sermon was beneficial and enjoyable. Lloyd-Jones's reply was, "Thank you for your word of encouragement. Very few people say such things to me."[13]

A person's basic yearning to be commended is not fundamentally unhealthy but wholesome—not sinful, but virtuous. Consider the following truths about our need for commendation.

First, it is rooted in our being created in the image of God. Wanting to have our performance evaluated as "very good" can be traced back to the personality of our heavenly Creator and Father in the six days of His work, and we are to imitate Him with the six days of our work (Gen. 1:4, 10, 12, 18, 21, 25, 31; 2:15). We were wired to thrive on commendation from the beginning in creation.

Second, it is rooted in our one day giving an account to God. As Christians who are new creations in Christ, we strive with longing to hear commendation from Him when we finally arrive home: "Well done, good and faithful servant" (Matt. 25:21, 23).

Third, it is rooted in our desire to hear, on the way home, from our fellow image bearers echoes of our heavenly Father's voice: "You are My beloved Son; in You I am well pleased" (Luke 3:22).

Fourth, it is to be restrained by our aspiration that sighs, "Not unto us, O LORD, not unto us, but to Your name give glory" (Ps. 115:1). It is not necessary that we shout "Glory to God!" every time we are commended. But though we might not always shout it, we should always think it.

Fifth, it is to be saturated with the humble recognition that anything good done by us or seen in us finds its origin in our heavenly Father: "Every good gift and every perfect gift is from above, and comes down from the Father of lights, with whom there is no variation or shadow of turning" (James 1:17).

Finally, it is to be restricted to seeking commendation for God-approved endeavors. Only what He calls good qualifies as worthy

---

13. Derick Bingham, *Encouragement: The Oxygen of the Soul* (Fearn, Scotland: Christian Focus, 1997), 33.

of our striving after and our being encouraged toward: "Beloved, do not imitate what is evil, but what is good. He who does good is of God, but he who does evil has not seen God" (3 John 11).

Keeping in mind these considerations, we shouldn't villainize commending encouragement as scratching people's pride itch any more than we would villainize romancing because it scratches a creature worship itch; mothering because it scratches a child idolatry itch; learning because it scratches a conceit itch; laboring because it scratches a workaholic itch; saving because it scratches a miser itch; or exercising because it scratches a narcissism itch.

Steve Douglas was in the television booth giving the stride-by-stride commentary for the Bannister-Landy miracle mile. Everyone wondered if the two could keep up the sizzling pace. But on the last lap, Douglas noted the rising thunder from the stadium: "There's beginning to come from the crowd a constant roar of approval and encouragement to their particular favorite." Both runners were getting shots of adrenaline. Both were spurred on by the spectators. And both broke the sub-four-minute-mile mark!

We are in the crowd of witnesses watching our neighbors run their lifelong races. Sitting in the stands, we may feel inhibitions that keep us silent and disinclinations to shout out cheers of encouragement. But we have a holy obligation to get up and roar with our lungs, giving shots of adrenaline with our words so that our striding friends might run with endurance the race set out before them (Heb. 12:1). As the apostle Paul says, "Encourage one another" (1 Thess. 5:11 NASB).

8

The Marriage Implications of
ENCOURAGEMENT

The love and affirmation of your spouse has the power to heal you of many of the deepest wounds. Why? If all the world says you are ugly, but your spouse says you are beautiful, you feel beautiful.
—Tim Keller

In a British period drama set in the early twentieth century, a local farmer, Mr. Drake, comes down with a case of dropsy, otherwise known as congestive heart failure, and becomes a patient of the small-town doctor. Poor Mrs. Drake looks on as her husband progressively swells up with excess fluid, particularly around his heart. Death seems inevitable—but who will take care of her and her several young children, who are now staring at a life without a husband and father? A nurse recommends to the doctor an innovative but risky surgical procedure that might save his life. It enlists the controversial substance adrenaline. Nearly widowed and desperate, Mrs. Drake approves the procedure.

A rare vial of adrenaline is ordered and arrives from London. The doctor then pierces Mr. Drake's chest cavity with an enormous needle and begins to quickly drain off pints of heart-drowning fluid. As expected, this stress to the heart induces a cardiac arrest, and Mr. Drake's heart stops beating. The nurse then calmly hands to the doctor a syringe of adrenaline, which is injected directly to the heart area. The adrenaline acts as a cardiac jump starter, and Mr. Drake's heart almost instantly springs into a healthy heartbeat again! Adrenaline was the life-restoring invigorator. And the entire Drake household was the beneficiary.

Encouragement is adrenaline. And in healthy households it shouldn't be used only as an exotic delicacy. It should be on tap as part of the daily family diet. It brings a healthy pulse to the whole household. In this chapter we will consider its implications for marriage.

Husbanding

A famine of encouragement can bring a marriage to cardiac arrest. An article in *The Atlantic*, "Masters of Love," reported on the four decades of research psychologist John Gottman conducted on thousands of couples to discover what makes relationships work. The esteemed Gottman Institute set up a "Love Lab," brought in newlywed couples, hooked them up to electrodes, and asked them to discuss the health of their relationships. During their discussions, the electrodes measured the couples' blood flow, heart rates, and sweat production. The couples then went home, and researchers contacted them six years later to find out if they were still married.

As the researchers studied the data they had gathered, they found two distinct groups: the "masters," who were still married after six years, and the "disasters," who had either ended their marriages or were miserably unhappy in them. The disasters had appeared calm during their interviews, but the electrodes recorded something different in their physiology. "Their heart rates were quick, their sweat glands were active, and their blood flow was fast." The couples who demonstrated a more active physiology were more aggressive toward each other, "showed signs of being in fight-or-flight mode.... Conversing with their spouse was, to their bodies, like facing off with a saber-toothed tiger," and their relationships deteriorated more quickly.

But the "masters" were calm, both outwardly and physiologically. They were loving and warm toward each other, even in times of conflict. Gottman's explanation:

"There's a habit of mind that the masters have," Gottman explained in an interview, "which is this: they are scanning social environment for things they can appreciate and say thank you for. They are building this culture of respect and appreciation very purposefully. Disasters are scanning the social environment for partners' mistakes."

"It's not just scanning environment," chimed in Julie Gottman. "It's scanning the partner for what the partner is doing right or scanning him for what he's doing wrong and criticizing versus respecting him and expressing appreciation." Contempt, they have found, is the number one factor that tears couples apart. People who are focused on criticizing their partners miss a whopping 50 percent of positive things their partners are doing and they see negativity when it's not there.[1]

The findings of the "Love Lab" convict me as a critical husband! When Dianne and I got married in 1982, our delightfully memorable honeymoon was stained with conflict. She spent so much time saying farewell to her bridesmaids and sisters that our getaway from Iowa was hours later than expected. She was selective about the restaurant we chose in Niagara Falls. I sat with her on a bench on a flowery Toronto boulevard and lectured her that I was the leader in our relationship and that she needed to be willing to follow. And after watching a Shakespeare play in Stratford, we quarreled about some difference of opinion I can't even remember. The bottom line for me was that I perceived in Dianne flaws (as if I were Mr. Perfect), and I was going to fix them by criticizing and correcting her. I prided myself in transparency and confrontation.

Nineteen years later when my dad died suddenly, I was stunned, staggered, and saddened by the great loss. The brevity of life smacked me in the face. My darling Dianne lay beside me in our bed. She had been such a fountain of blessing and goodness to me over nearly two decades. I mused, "Am I wise to spend the precious

---

1. Emily Esfahani Smith, "Masters of Love," *The Atlantic*," June 12, 2014, https://www.theatlantic.com/health/archive/2014/06/happily-ever-after/372573/.

few moments we have together in our fleeting lives circling around perceived quirks and flaws? Life is too short, Mark! Let it go! Don't obsess on her blemishes. Bask in her virtues." That night I made a quantum leap forward in wise and loving husbanding.

Paul tells husbands to love their wives "as Christ also loved the church" (Eph. 5:25) and as they love their "own bodies.... He who loves his wife loves himself" (v. 28). Charles Hodge perceptively writes:

> Marital love, therefore, is as much a dictate of nature as self-love; and it is just as unnatural for a man to hate his wife, as it would be for him to hate himself, or his own body. A man may have a body which does not altogether suit him. He may wish it were handsomer, healthier, stronger, or more active. Still it is his body, it is himself; and he nourishes it and cherishes it as tenderly as though it were the best and loveliest a man ever had. So a man may have a wife whom he could wish to be better, or more beautiful, or more agreeable; still she is his wife, and by the constitution of nature and ordinance of God, a part of himself. In neglecting or abusing her he violates the laws of nature as well as the law of God. It is thus Paul presents the matter.[2]

As my own scarred, blemished, odd-looking, flawed body naturally gets daily pampering and primping from me, my precious bride deserves the same royal, tender treatment. In the famous love chapter, 1 Corinthians 13, the apostle Paul describes the love husbands should show to their wives: "Love suffers long and is kind; love does not envy; love does not parade itself, is not puffed up; does not behave rudely, does not seek its own, is not provoked, thinks no evil; does not rejoice in iniquity, but rejoices in the truth; bears all things, believes all things, hopes all things, endures all things" (vv. 4–7).

---

2. Charles Hodge, *A Commentary on the Epistle to the Ephesians* (Grand Rapids: Baker, 1980), 336.

Dianne is like an exquisite and delicate vase who deserves my honoring and polishing and encouraging, not my belittling and rough handling and criticizing. Peter elaborates:

> Husbands, likewise, dwell with them with understanding, giving honor to the wife, as to the weaker vessel, and as being heirs together of the grace of life, that your prayers may not be hindered.
>
> Finally, all of you be of one mind, having compassion for one another; love as brothers, be tenderhearted, be courteous; not returning evil for evil or reviling for reviling, but on the contrary blessing, knowing that you were called to this, that you may inherit a blessing. (1 Peter 3:7–9)

For husbands, surely there is still a place for loving confrontation. But they need to dial it down and pick their battles. They must take on the personality of an encourager and put off the persona of a faultfinder. Husbands should be Proverbs 31 men: "Her children rise up and call her blessed; her husband also, and he praises her" (v. 28).

Husbands need to take a page out of Solomon's husbanding manual, his Song. They must be heavy on affectionate and affirming encouragement. They should find the good and overlook the not-so-good. In Song of Solomon, the exemplary groom is extravagant in loving his bride with words of encouragement, compliment, and affirmation:

> Behold, you are fair, my love!
> Behold, you are fair!
> You have dove's eyes. (1:15)

> Your teeth are like a flock of shorn sheep
> Which have come up from the washing,
> Every one of which bears twins,
> And none is barren among them. (4:2)

Solomon basks in the fact that his beautiful bride still has all her teeth—a stunning feature one thousand years ago! He's ever scanning her life for things worthy of his appreciation, and he verbally expresses what it is about her that delights him: "You are all fair, my love, and there is no spot in you" (4:7). "My dove, my perfect one, is the only one [like you]" (6:9).

A few years ago, Dianne got away for a couple of days, spending some time with her sisters. This left me home alone with our five children. We were fine for the first few hours. But then we all instinctively began to wonder when she would come back and glanced longingly out the front window, looking for her return. Yes, without her animated nurturing we were still a family, but we had lost our soul. When she returned, I buried her in an embrace and told her, "Without you, Babe, our Technicolor family is reduced to black and white!" I hope I'm learning.

Wifing

Mrs. Drake, whom we encountered at the beginning of this chapter, wisely helped her husband by seeing that he received strengthening adrenaline. The heroic, life-saving action she took for her husband epitomizes well her God-assigned role as a "helper suitable": And the LORD God said, "It is not good that man should be alone; I will make him a helper comparable [suitable, NASB] to him" (Gen. 2:18). The term *helper* is the Hebrew word *ezer*, which means "strength giver."

The old hymn "Come Thou Fount of Every Blessing" has these familiar lines, which include the word *Ebenezer*, coming from *ezer*:

> Here I raise my Ebenezer;
> Hither by thy help I've come;
> And I hope, by thy good pleasure,
> Safely to arrive at home.

The Lord helped Israel conquer the Philistines, so they called him their Eben-*ezer*—stone of help (1 Sam. 7:10–12). The wife is to help her husband conquer the foes of life, so she is called a "helper suitable." Some wives fail to strengthen their husbands by infusing strengthening adrenaline and inadvertently hurt them by overexposing them to weakening "Kryptonite" (Superman's point of vulnerability).

In her book *Fierce Woman: The Power of a Soft Warrior*, Kimberly Wagner confesses how she, a high-octane woman, grew disillusioned with her husband's flawed leadership in their marriage. Her husband, the pastor of a flourishing church, just didn't measure up. Wagner was critical, intimidating, and impatient, leaving her husband feeling like he couldn't do anything right, so that he spiraled into discouragement. Wagner reveals, "I was repulsed by his depression. He needed to get his act together, to be a man." Her husband stunned her by resigning from the pastorate. This was a wake-up call to her. The Lord convicted Wagner through 1 Peter 3:1–6 that she hadn't been a "gentle and quiet" helper, but rather a brash and loud hurter. Retrospectively analyzing her early marriage years, she recognized how she had harshly countered her husband's leadership with her "superior" plan, her hypercritical spirit, and her take-charge personality. She had systematically emasculated him.[3]

Wagner is not alone in her critical spirit. In confessing her own critical wifely tendencies, Martha Peace hit the mark by saying that "as [her husband's] helpmeet, he needs my helpful suggestions and not my sarcastic putdowns."[4] For a wife, a crucial battle is fighting the common plague of critical and disrespectful talk to her husband. Proverbs makes no little thing of this besetting sin of belittling wifely speech:

> Better to dwell in a corner of a housetop,
> Than in a house shared with a contentious woman.
> (21:9; 25:24)

> Better to dwell in the wilderness,
> Than with a contentious and angry woman. (21:19)

---

3. Kimberly Wagner, *Fierce Women: The Power of a Soft Warrior* (Chicago: Moody, 2012), 97–98.

4. Martha Peace, *The Excellent Wife: A Biblical Perspective* (Bemidji, Minn.: Focus, 1995), 107.

> A continual dripping on a very rainy day
> And a contentious woman are alike. (27:15)

A husband needs his wife to be the reviving corner in the fight of life. You've seen boxers getting pummeled in the ring, but at the round's end they retreat to their corner for reinvigorating encouragement and refreshment. The exhausted boxer hears things like this: "Okay, you took some hits. But you delivered some good ones too. You are the man! You have what it takes to get back out there and take down that Goliath!" Wives are to be that strengthening corner in their husbands' life. And the adrenaline of encouragement is a crucial ingredient to their helper coaching: "Therefore comfort [encourage, NASB] each other and edify one another, just as you also are doing" (1 Thess. 5:11).

A husband comes home to his wife and retreats to his corner, often bruised and beaten. He doesn't need the Kryptonite of a critical spirit, but the adrenaline of a cheering encourager. Wives must be helpers with their words, not hurters.

Some wives often act like Eve, who was enticed into destroying her marriage and her world by a craving for more. God had nestled her comfortably in a paradise stocked with unimaginable plenty, including trees with low-hanging sweet fruit and a good—even very good—husband. But Paradise wasn't enough. Eve wanted more. It is that seed of dissatisfaction that the serpent craftily watered, saying to the woman, "Has God indeed said, 'You shall not eat of every tree of the garden'?" (Gen. 3:1). He hissed the insinuation that God was stingily restricting her from something better.

Kim Wagner writes, "Eve's ingratitude took her from the lush gardens of peaceful contentment and drove her into the wilderness of desolate places: always seeking; painful longing; insatiable hunger; empty dreams.... While in the car driving to my first meeting with Anne [a girlfriend involved in a forbidden fruit affair because her husband Gary failed to gratify her emotional needs], I called my husband to have him pray for me. Before I hung up, I asked him to give me one word from a husband's perspective; one word of counsel that I might need to give to Anne. The word he spoke was *gratitude.*"[5] Dr. Laura Schlessinger's book *The Proper Care and Feeding of Husbands* grew out of her receiving and evaluating thousands of comments from men all around the country. In her chapter titled "You're a Nag," she wrote, "The universal complaint of men who e-mailed my Web site with their opinions about *The Proper Care and Feeding of Husbands* was that their wives criticize, complain, nag, rarely compliment or express appreciation, are difficult to satisfy, and basically not as nice to them as they'd be to a stranger ringing their doorbell at three A.M.!"[6]

Many men divulged how they were esteemed as competent professionals by their colleagues but were treated by their wives as being frequently incompetent. Jim wrote, "I have always had superlative evaluations on my performance. AT HOME, I CAN'T DO ANYTHING RIGHT! I sometimes spend several minutes in thought on a task at hand, trying to decide exactly what to do. After weighing the pros and cons, I make a decision and act. Almost invariably I get, "What did you do that for? Now I can't...," or I hear, "Who put the ??? here?" or sometimes I get a straight-out "That's stupid."... It's something that wears you down like erosion."[7]

Happily, most wives are not so critical of their husbands, but discouraging talk can make a man's home a "Kryptonite corner." Wives should know there is a great upside to the wise bridling and kind use of their tongues: "A wholesome [soothing, NASB] tongue is a tree of life" (Prov. 15:4). Kind and encouraging words from a wife to a husband are adrenaline. They send him back into the ring singing instead of sulking.

It is interesting how the Lord got a song out of Adam by giving him Eve. Remember that after a time God declared, "It is not good that man should be alone; I will make him a helper comparable

---

5. Wagner, *Fierce Women,* 79–80.

6. Laura Schlessinger, *The Proper Care and Feeding of Husbands* (New York: Harper, 2006), 37–38.

7. Schlessinger, *The Proper Care and Feeding of Husbands,* 40.

[suitable, NASB] to him" (Gen. 2:18). And after the man wakes up and beholds his tailor-made wife, we read the first recorded words of a man, and they come out in the form of a poetic song:

> This is now bone of my bones
> And flesh of my flesh;
> She shall be called Woman,
> Because she was taken out of Man. (Gen. 2:23)

It takes a woman to get the song out of the man! Men desperately need their wives. Church elder, writer, and publisher Matthew Jacobson addresses wives:

> Do you truly understand the immense power you have in the life of your husband? *Every Wife is a King Maker. She has the power to build him up or tear him down. How will you use your power today?*
>
> From the man's perspective, if his woman doesn't believe in him…isn't fanatically committed to his potential, it doesn't much matter what others think….
>
> *We need your affirmation—we have to have it and, oh, how we thrive with it.* Typically, men are quiet about these things but that doesn't mean we need and enjoy our wife's affirmation any less. And every man feels it: When his woman is behind him, he can slay dragons.[8]

Tim and Kathy Keller perceptively explain the peculiar power of a wife as helper (ezer) and strength giver:

> In my own life, I must confess that I had never felt "manly" until I got married. I was a nerd before it was fashionable, playing trumpet in the marching band and staying in the Boy Scouts through high school. Good things, no doubt, but not cool or macho. I was often mocked and excluded, especially during high school, for my uncoolness. But Kathy looked at

---

8. Matthew Jacobson, "103 Words of Affirmation Every Husband Wants to Hear," Faithful Man, accessed May 29, 2018, https://faithfulman.com/103-words-of -affirmation-every-husbands-wants-to-hear/. Words in italics for emphasis were originally in boldface type.

me like her knight in shining armor. She has always told me, and continues to tell me, that though all the world may look at me and see Clark Kent, she knows that underneath I have on blue underwear. She has always been very quick to point out and celebrate anything I have done that is courageous. Over the years, bit by bit, it has sunk in. To my wife, I'm Superman, and it makes me feel like a man in a way nothing else could.[9]

Kim Wagner asks, "Do you brag on him to his face and to others in front of him? Do you let him know specific ways you are proud of him? Do you affirm him for making difficult choices? Do you remind him of things he's done well when he's struggling with fear of failure?... As I began doing that, I was amazed. I hadn't realized how much men need the wife's positive reinforcement. It's like fuel for their motor."[10]

Gary Chapman reports that he met with Bill and Betty Jo in Little Rock, Arkansas, after a seminar he had given. He had only one hour to help them. After twelve years and two children, their marriage was in a shambles. They disagreed on everything and wondered why they ever got married in the first place. Bill's chief complaint was, "There is simply no affection coming from her. I work my butt off and there is simply no appreciation." Betty Jo sighed. "He's an excellent provider, but he does nothing around the house to help me, and never has time for me." Chapman had one word of advice for Betty Jo. He encouraged her to think hard and come up with a list of legitimate positive traits of Bill. She did:

1. He hasn't missed a day in twelve years. He's aggressive in his work. 2. He's received several promotions through the years, and is always thinking of ways to improve his productivity. 3. He makes the house payment each month. 4. He pays the

---

9. Timothy Keller with Kathy Keller, *The Meaning of Marriage: Facing the Complexities of Commitment with the Wisdom of God* (New York: Dutton, 2011), 147–48.

10. Wagner, *Fierce Women*, 127.

gas, electrical, and water bill. 5. He bought us a recreational vehicle three years ago. 5. He mows the grass and rakes the leaves. 6. He provides plenty of money for food and clothing. 6. He carries out the garbage once a month. 7. He provides money for me to provide Christmas presents for the family. 8. He agrees that I can use the money I make at my part-time job any way I desire.

Chapman urged Betty Jo to experiment, to keep looking for Bill's virtues, and then verbally express appreciation in a timely fashion. After two months, Chapman called Bill and asked if the marital climate had changed. Bill's response was, "She has actually made me feel like a man again. We've got a ways to go, Dr. Chapman, but I really believe we're on the road."[11]

Sweet encouragement by far outperforms bitter nagging. Imagine this scenario: A wife wants the trash taken out after dinner. She could nag her husband every five minutes about it. And then when he finally takes care of it, she might mumble, "It's about time."

Or there is another scenario: A wife could sweetly say, "Honey, I've put the bag by the door for you. When you have time, could you take it out to the garage and throw it into the dumpster?" And then when her husband does it, she can catch him on the way back into the house, wrap her arms around him, give him a big kiss, and with a twinkle in her eye, tell him how hard it is for her to lift that dumpster lid with one arm and then lift that heavy bag with the other. Then she can say, "You're sweet, Babe." That wife has just made her Clark Kent into Superman. Adrenaline is much better than Kryptonite. A husband wants an encouraging, admiring bride, not one who criticizes and belittles him. Wives need to respect their husbands with their words. The Lord will smile on such marriages: "Nevertheless let each one of you in particular so love his own wife as himself, and let the wife see that she respects her husband" (Eph. 5:33).

---

11. Gary D. Chapman, *The Five Love Languages: The Secret to Love That Lasts* (Chicago: Northfield Publishing, 2015), 50.

The story of Kim and Leroy Wagner has a happy ending. Leroy writes appreciatively of Kim, his improved, sweetened, and softened warrior wife:

> Where at one point I was so paralyzed by fear that I wouldn't even make a decision because I knew there could be repercussions or negative consequences, now I don't fear a reprisal. Now I have the freedom to go to God, to pray, to lead, and even if it doesn't turn out to be the greatest decision, if I fumble or drop the ball in some way, I know that Kim will say, "Well, you're still my man, and we'll trust the Lord together." I know that she'll give encouragement. I once thought our marriage was going to crush us both, be the death of me, but now we experience freedom and joy in our relationship. It is a safe place.[12]

Kim, the fiercely criticizing and weakening hurter, had become a fiercely encouraging and strengthening helper.

In conclusion, Tim Keller's words sum up well the marital implications of encouragement in both husbanding and wifing:

> Marriage puts into your spouse's hand a massive power to reprogram your own self-appreciation. He or she can overturn anything previously said about you, to a great degree redeeming the past. The love and affirmation of your spouse has the power to heal you of many of the deepest wounds. Why? If all the world says you are ugly, but your spouse says you are beautiful, you feel beautiful....
>
> The same aspect of what entails the power of truth also contributes to this power of love. That is, because marriage merges two lives and brings you into the closest possible contact, a positive assessment by your spouse has ultimate credibility. If someone I know a little comes up to me and says, "You are one of the kindest men I know," I will certainly feel complimented and pleased. But how deeply will it sink

---

12. Wagner, *Fierce Women*, 132–33.

in? Not too far. Why? Because a part of my heart says, "Well nice. But he doesn't really know me at all." But if my wife, after years of living with me, says, "You are one of the kindest men I know," that goes in. The affirmation is profoundly comforting. Why? Because she knows me better than anyone. And if over the years, you have grown to love and admire your spouse more and more, then his or her praise will get more and more strengthening and healing.[13]

May the Lord Jesus give us grace to be daily dispensers of adrenaline-like encouragement to our spouses, bringing a healthy and strong pulse to our marriages.

---

13. Keller, *Meaning of Marriage*, 147–49.

9

The Parenting Implications of
ENCOURAGEMENT

Nothing can more discourage a child than a spirit of incessant fault-finding, on the part of its parent.

—John Abbott

The Lord has given to parents an almost disturbing dictatorial rule over their children. The fifth commandment reads, "Honor your father and your mother" (Ex. 20:12). This gives parents sway over their little ones like nothing else. God solemnly obligates children to "honor" their parents. It is the Hebrew word *cavad*, which fundamentally means "take as heavy." In other words, children are not to disrespectfully treat their parents' words as lightweight feathers that don't budge them, but like heavyweight sandbags that morally and spiritually move them. Children are to allow their parents' words to move them, direct them, influence them, and impact them. This makes the honoring child vulnerable and the honorable parents careful—to select words that are true and not false, kind and not cruel, life-giving and not soul-crushing. Parents should strive to encourage.

Fathering

Dr. James Dobson reminisced about the imperfections of his father:

> I remember working with him one day in the back yard when I was 15 years of age, on a day when he was particularly irritable for some reason. He just crabbed at me for everything I did, even when I hustled. Finally, he yelled at me

for something I considered petty and I just threw down the rake and I quit—I just walked off. And I walked across our property and down the street while my dad demanded that I come back. It was one of the few times in my life that I ever took him on like that! Well, I meandered around town for a while, wondering what would happen to me when I finally went home. And I ended up at my cousin's house on the other side of town. After several hours there, with knees quaking, I called home. "Stay there," said my dad, "I'm coming over." To say that I was nervous would be a gross understatement. In a short time Dad arrived and asked to see me alone. "Bo," he began. "I didn't treat you right this afternoon. I was riding your back for no good reason and I want you to know I'm sorry. Your mom and I want you to come home now." It was a difficult moment for him, but he made a friend for life.[1]

I wish I could say that critical, crabby irritability has never stained my fatherhood, but I know it did. In fact, it is a besetting fault for many dads. The key note of fathers shouldn't be critical irritability, but encouraging harmony. The first recorded words between our begetting heavenly Father and His beloved Son are full of significance and instruction: "When He had been baptized, Jesus came up immediately from the water; and behold, the heavens were opened to Him, and He saw the Spirit of God descending like a dove and alighting upon Him. And suddenly a voice came from heaven, saying, 'This is My beloved Son, in whom I am well pleased'" (Matt. 3:16–17). Pastor, writer, and apologist Doug Wilson observes:

> There is a world of information about fatherhood in these two brief verses. First, when Jesus was baptized, His Father was there. Second, He made His presence felt by sending His Spirit to descend like a dove in order to rest upon Jesus. Third,

---

1. James Dobson, "The Day My Dad Apologized," *Dr. James Dobson's Family Talk*, accessed May 29, 2018, http://www.drjamesdobson.org/Broadcasts /Broadcast?i=fea5aba5-4c0a-4224-995f-4720bd0195a8#.

He made His presence known by speaking. And so what did He say?… He said, "This is my Son." Fourth, He expressed His love for His Son—"This is my beloved Son." And last, He expressed His pleasure in His Son. The first thing we are told about the relationship of the Father to the Son is that the Father thought His Son was doing a great job.[2]

You may protest, "My child doesn't measure up to the virtue of Jesus!" I understand. None of us measure up either. But our heavenly Father daily throws us circumstantial kisses and whispers scriptural encouragements, and on the last day, He'll crown us by saying, "Well done, good and faithful servant" (Matt. 25:21, 23).

Yes, fathers must reprimand, rebuke, and discipline ("without chastening…then you are illegitimate and not sons," Heb. 12:8), but we need to resist our tendency to be excessive faultfinders. In training our children to strive for excellence, we can become abrasive, white-glove-reprimanding drill sergeants hypercritically evaluating. Fathers can be guilty of making comments like these:

- She speaks with a bit of a lisp.
- He can't tie his shoes yet, so they stay untied.
- Her hair is wrong.
- He slept too long.
- She doesn't sit in a ladylike way.
- He mumbles instead of speaking clearly.
- She talks with her mouth full.
- He puts way too much syrup on his waffles.

Like Dr. Dobson's dad, fathers can be constantly badgering and nitpicking.

But Scripture gives a different picture of how fathers ought to behave toward their children:

2. Douglas Wilson, *Father Hunger: Why God Calls Men to Love and Lead Their Families* (Nashville: Thomas Nelson, 2012), 2.

Fathers, do not provoke your children to wrath. (Eph. 6:4)

Fathers, do not provoke [exasperate, NASB] your children, lest they become discouraged. (Col. 3:21)

A sour tone that is provoking and exasperating is relationally corrosive. We can usually hear it better in others than we can in ourselves. I can remember, as a younger father, hearing that sourness in a pastor friend of mine. It was in the way he talked to his son. The two would verbally spar, and I heard little sweetness and a lot of bitter. The dad seemed to interpret almost everything his son did and said from the darkest angle. His tone was not pleasurable, but adversarial. Over the years, the relationship seemingly never got out of that rut, and the rest is a sour history. The son went off to the far country. I know that I have been rutted into that tone, and typically my helping wife has recognized it, told me about it, and thrown me a rope to pull me out of it.

When Sam Crabtree, a pastor at Bethlehem Baptist Church in Minneapolis, Minnesota, lectured at a seminar for a Campus Crusade staff on the benefits of building up others by praise and affirmation, he noticed that during the second session, one man's chair was conspicuously empty. Later, the man sought out Crabtree with an explanation for his absence:

I'm sorry I missed your next session. But after you talked about praising and affirming, I went to the phone. I have a 14 year old son who hasn't spoken to me for about two years. We used to fight about almost everything, and over time, the fighting dissolved into a long, silent, uneasy truce. After being convicted by this teaching on affirmation, I called him, resolute that I wasn't going to criticize or correct him in any way, but praise him, because I do see things in him that are commendable. Well, this son who hasn't said boo to me in two years talked to me for 45 minutes! I wasn't going to hang up. That's why I missed that session.[3]

Encouragement is adrenaline. Well-timed doses of it spur children on to maturity by putting away childish things in pursuing manhood and womanhood. That's just what we want. We want them to reach toward greatness. So when your son spontaneously decides to wash the family van and you spy a dirt stripe he missed on the driver-side door panel, it is probably not time to critically nitpick about the streak but resoundingly applaud the wash effort. We want our children to reach daringly. Common sense teaches us that if we slap their hand every time they attempt to serve in some way, they'll be gun-shy to even try.

During my teen years, I worked in the pro shop of an elite golf country club. Don was the assistant pro, and he stood well over six feet tall, had an intimidating low voice, and could hit the ball a mile. It was tough working for Don when he was supervising us pro shop workers. Don drove us by withering criticism. He'd bark, "Who strapped McInerney's clubs on the passenger side of the golf cart? Everyone knows Mac always wants to drive!" Or, "Why are there still grass stains on Gillette's pitching wedge?" Don's criticisms would continue like that throughout the day. Under Don's critical gaze, I was always tense, lacking confidence, and moving slowly in fear of making a mistake that would cost me a verbal lashing.

But when Don was off playing golf somewhere, Tom was in charge. Tom was the caddy master. Tom drove us by encouragement: "How did you get all those carts bagged and parked so fast?" "I like the way you lined them up along the sidewalk in formation. Looks like F-16 fighter planes ready to fly off on a mission." "I think you plucked clean all those balls from the driving range in near record time!" With Tom's encouragements I was always

---

3. Sam Crabtree, *Practicing Affirmation: God-Centered Praise of Those Who Are Not God* (Wheaton, Ill.: Crossway, 2011), 35–36.

relaxed, confident, creative, and motivated to work as I anticipated praise for a good job.

In 1833, pastor and author John Abbott wrote on parenting:

> It is at times necessary to censure and to punish. But very much may be done by encouraging children when they do well. Be even more careful to express your approval of good conduct, than your disapproval of bad. Nothing can more discourage a child than a spirit of incessant fault-finding, on the part of its parent.... There are two great motives influencing human actions—hope and fear. Both of these are at times necessary. But who would not prefer to have his child influenced to good conduct by the desire of pleasing, rather than by the fear of offending. If a parent never expresses gratification when the children do well, and is always censuring when seeing anything amiss, they are discouraged and unhappy. They feel that there is no use in trying to please.... At last, finding that, whether they do good or bad, they are equally found fault with, they quit all efforts to please, and become hardened to the chronic criticism.[4]

Once when I was golfing with my friend Bruce, I noticed that he paused before climbing out of the cart and sent a brief text to his college-age daughter on a faraway campus. He paused to explain, "I told her I was thinking of her and that I love her. It is like drip irrigation. She thrives on my daily spoonfuls of affirmation."

I know from experience that children do many foolish things. But as a child of God, so do I, and my heavenly Father is so kind to hourly embrace me with long-suffering patience. It is like drip irrigation. Right now I'm enjoying God's encouragement as I sit in my Michigan backyard under a shade tree in late June. It is 74 degrees, with a gentle breeze, and there are no clouds in the sky— and no snow in the near forecast! Daily, our Father undeservedly blesses us!

---

4. John S. C. Abbott, *The Mother at Home, or, The Principles of Maternal Duty: Familiarly Illustrated* (New York: American Tract Society, 1833), 102.

Mothering

Mothers have it tougher. Supervising the children all the time can be a Chinese water torture test for even the most patient moms. There is so much to correct! And an excellent wife of Proverbs 31 is task oriented (rising early, preparing food, making clothes, buying a field), isn't she? A woman trying to meet a demanding daily to-do list does not easily suffer fools. But a crucial ingredient in the mother whose "children rise up and call her blessed" (Prov. 31:28) is "on her tongue is the law of kindness" (v. 26). Moms need to resist chronic fault-finding in their children. Just like the woman of Proverbs 31, mothers themselves thrive on praise: "Give her of the fruit of her hands, and let her own works praise her in the gates" (v. 31). And wise moms feed praise like this to their children too.

Moms should seek out things to praise. They should splash their children throughout the day not with frowns and scowls, but with smiles and winks. At the end of an especially good day, a mom can commend her young son, "You've been a really good boy today. It makes my heart sing when you act so wisely!" She should kiss him on the forehead, turn out the lights, and leave him with a simple resolution to try his best tomorrow.

Basil Hall tells of two alternating ship commanders aboard the same vessel. Whenever one would board, he'd make his after-breakfast rounds scanning the decks to detect the smallest thing out of place and grumble about it. Seeing a half an inch of boat yarn on a deck white as snow, he'd growl: "I wish you'd teach these sweepers to clear away that rope debris!" He acted this way on principle, thinking his crusty criticism was the best preventative to neglect on the part of the crew.

The other commander could make the same stroll, but remark, "How white and clean you've gotten these decks today! I think you must have been at them all morning, to have got them in such order." Hall noted: "Under the one, we all worked with cheerfulness, from a conviction that nothing we did in a proper way would miss his approval. But our duty under the other, being performed in fear, seldom went on with much spirit. We had no personal satisfaction in doing things correctly, from the certainty of getting no commendation."[5]

Sons require special treatment. Men, both young and old, thrive on being recognized as courageous, brave, and valiant. It is emboldening for a son to hear words from his mother that communicate, "You're my hero!" instead of "You're such a wimp!"

King David made sure to record and publish the names and deeds of his mighty men (see 2 Samuel 23), probably believing that such recognition would inspire them to even greater feats of valor. He was even careful to heap commendation not only on spectacular exploits like killing a lion in a pit on a snowy day (v. 20) but also for mundane duties like guarding the baggage behind the battle lines (1 Sam. 30:24). In so doing, he lionized his men. Parents must lionize their sons by dignifying them with at least a junior level of respect so they can one day grow into the senior level (Eph. 5:33).

Parents should commend their sons for doing noble things like getting the mail in a blizzard, shoveling heavy or deep snow, emptying the mousetrap, walking home into the teeth of a frigid wind, and staining the deck on a sweltering afternoon. They should cloak their sons with respect in their childhood, and their sons will seek to grow into it in their manhood. Parents should teach their sons how to deserve, receive, and handle respect. They must beware of lavishing praise apart from genuine accomplishment and should not detach commendation from true achievement. Sons will learn to disregard that kind of praising as patronizing.

Daughters also require special treatment. I've coached the soccer teams of my four sons and one daughter. I've discovered that the boys do best on a ratio of about 4:1 encouragement versus reprimand. The girls' ratio is more like 8:1. They are just wonderfully different!

---

5. Abbott, *Mother at Home*, 66–67.

Author Nancy Wilson speaks from maternal experience:

The first thing mothers must remember in raising young women is to be kind. A critical spirit is a destructive thing, and mothers must not be too hard on their girls. Mothers are naturally prone to be easier on the guys, but this must not be. Mothers must not attribute motives to their daughters, not take offense, nor lose patience, not take things personally as they are raising their daughters. Rather they should put on tender mercies.... Daughters primarily need love and security. This is why a critical spirit is so destructive. Remember, we want our children to have fat, prospering souls. Criticism and impatience destroy rather than build up. Daughters need to feel important, loved, accepted, needed, wanted, and appreciated. Mothers must be diligent to praise their daughters.[6]

Sam Crabtree tells the story of his eleven-year-old daughter. He and his wife felt like they were losing her, like almost overnight she thought her parents' brains were sucked empty of anything valuable. The silence and alienation momentum was bad and forecast an even worse teenage era. So Sam began a careful study of his daughter to rescue her:

As I entered her room that day, I noticed that she had arranged the items on the top of her dresser in such a way that the taller things were in the back row, and shorter things were stair-stepped toward the front, so that you could see everything.... I exclaimed, "I like what you've done here! You're methodical. This makes complete sense. Very orderly. Very systematized. I see the character of God in this."... And with that, I walked out ignoring the rest of the tsunami in her room. Only a few minutes later, I happened to walk past the kitchen when she was hugging her mom. I made affirming her my responsibility. I kept up the barrage of affirmations, and in

6. Nancy Wilson, *The Fruit of Her Hands: Respect and the Christian Woman*, rev. ed. (Moscow, Idaho: Canon Press, 1997), 66.

a matter of days we had our daughter back. To this very day…
the channels of communication are open and sweet.[7]

Grandparenting

George McDearmon is a man with a football-coach personality
who became a gifted pastor in upstate New York. He is a model
father. His only son, Greg, benefited wonderfully from his dad's
coach-like spurring him on to more excellent levels of manhood.
Greg, who played defensive free safety for his high school football
team, talks about the night he didn't play well in a big conference
rivalry game: "Afterward, Dad read me the riot act. He reminded
me of a third quarter play when the opposing tailback slipped by
me for a touchdown run, and scolded, 'Man, Greg, at least you
could have shaken his hand when he blew by you!'"

Years later, Greg moved to Louisville and had a son of his
own—Iain. When Iain was about three years old, Grandpa McDearmon visited Kentucky for a week. And every day, he took Iain for a
ride to a nearby ice-cream shop for a cone, just the two of them. At
week's end, Greg, in disbelief, teased, "This is unbelievable, Dad. I
could count on one hand the times you took me out for ice cream all
the years of my childhood, and here you've exceeded that with Iain
in a single week!" George calculatingly and perceptively responded,
"That's because, Greg, I'm *not* Iain's father, but his grandfather."

What George meant was that the role of a grandparent greatly
differs from the role of a parent. Parents are peculiarly assigned
by God to be the important chief heavies, the discipliners, punish-
ers, correctors, and rebukers in the lives of their children. Scripture
affirms this:

> He who spares his rod hates his son,
> But he who loves him disciplines him promptly.
> (Prov. 13:24)

---

7. Crabtree, *Practicing Affirmation*, 57–58.

> Chasten your son while there is hope,
> And do not set your heart on his destruction. (19:18)

> Correct your son, and he will give you rest;
> Yes, he will give delight to your soul. (29:17)

If you endure chastening, God deals with you as with sons; for what son is there whom a father does not chasten? But if you are without chastening, of which all have become partakers, then you are illegitimate and not sons. Furthermore, we have had human fathers who corrected us, and we paid them respect. Shall we not much more readily be in subjection to the Father of spirits and live? (Heb. 12:7–9)

Grandparents are not the heavies. Nature and Scripture teach us that grandparents are assigned more to be gracious and blessing benefactors than stern and disciplining rebukers:

> Then Israel [Jacob, grandfather to Joseph's sons] saw Joseph's sons, and said, "Who are these?"
> Joseph said to his father [Jacob], "They are my sons, whom God has given me in this place."
> And he said, "Please bring them to me, and I will bless them." (Gen. 48:8–9)

> A good man leaves an inheritance to his children's children. (Prov. 13:22)

This is an important concept because as we age, we can tend to become chronically cranky and constantly correcting critics of both our grandchildren and of their not-measuring-up-in-our-eyes parents. We can try to take up the rod of authority in our own hands. (It is true that in this generation of divorce and single-parent households, grandparents may be thrust into the role of daily parental caretaker. That's a different story.)

I've seen the tragic fallout of abrasively confronting grandparents burning bridges forever with their not-flying-right grandchildren. Instead of habitually serving up a refreshing talk with an ice-cream cone, they try frequently to force down bitter asparagus with a scolding reprimand. They must not do this.

My wife has been a great example to me as I transition from father to grandfather. Our toddler grandson Richard was once spending the day at our house. He was inconsolably crying for no reason in sight. My instincts were to bark out, "We don't do that here, Richard!" Dianne embodied the Christlike trait of "a bruised reed He will not break, and smoking flax [wick] He will not quench" (Matt. 12:20). She said, "Richard, talk to Grammy. What's the matter? You can tell me." Turns out he was really hungry, and a cup of yogurt transformed an emotional wreck into an adorable delight—normal Richard mode.

During one extended family dinner on a Sunday afternoon, Richard was in an uncharacteristically less-than-stellar and uncooperative mood. Richard's dad, our son Austin, calmly snatched him up and conducted a parental discipline session in a remote bedroom. The result was another wonderful transformation! On Monday morning, Dianne reminisced, "Austin did a great job at the table with Richard yesterday. He did all the right things!" I immediately texted Austin, "Mom said you were the man yesterday in wisely handling Richard." This was adrenaline to Daddy Austin.

I'm reminded of Austin's comments as the extended family sat reminiscing together in the afterglow of my dad's funeral. My dad had taken a special interest in Austin, who was born with a spina bifida deformity, taking him under his wing, going golfing with him one-on-one, cheering on his slowest grandson at his ball games, playing an incalculably formative and strengthening role in the boy's life. And yes, Papa Chanski did take Austin out for one-on-one ice cream. Knowing my very direct dad, he no doubt occasionally had an "Austin, step into my office" moment. But generally Dad left the serving up of the asparagus to me.

Thirteen-year-old Austin's funeral afterglow words were more profoundly epitomizing than anything anyone else said. Uncles and aunts and cousins remembered and laughed and cried together. Then Austin spoke: "Papa was always there." Silence. More silence.

Austin got it right. With those encouraging memories forever treasured away, my dad left a wealthy inheritance to his child's child. Papa Chanski was adrenaline to grandson Austin.

Austin's maternal Grandma Becker understands this concept too. She still has a way of serving up sharp and tart rhubarb surrounded in sweet pie a la mode. She sometimes quite directly and critically tells her grandchildren what she thinks, but she has a crafty way of serving it up with Dairy Queen sweetness. Yes, sometimes ice cream brings more invigorating health than asparagus. George McDearmon and other wise grandparents know it.

Giving encouragement is a shot of adrenaline. And in healthy households it shouldn't be used only as an exotic delicacy but as part of the daily family diet. It gives a healthy pulse to the entire family.

10

The Church and Therapeutic
ENCOURAGEMENT

When all things are fair in character, you're not to go motive hunting. It's better to be occasionally deceived, than to live always in a temperature of suspicion.

—William Jay

In his book *The Power of the Other: The Startling Effect Other People Have on You*, Henry Cloud tells of his Navy SEAL brother-in-law Mark—the brother he never had, the kind of brother every child wants—who was killed in the Iraq War. Mark became a Navy SEAL, one of those American heroes known for his strength, stamina, and grit in surviving BUD/S (Basic Underwater Demolition/ SEAL) training, a grueling endurance test that pushes already-at-the-top specimens to their absolute limits. More than two-thirds of the candidates don't make the cut and are disqualified.

In the aftermath of his brother-in-law's death, Cloud met many SEALs whose lives had been profoundly touched by Mark. He tells one story about a teammate he calls Bryce, who was swimming in the ocean during training week, approaching the finish line. Mark, who had already passed the final test and knew he would become a SEAL, watched his friends striving to make the goal. While Mark watched, Bryce's body gave out—he had nothing left to keep going. After years of dreaming about and training to become a Navy SEAL, Bryce began to sink. As he was on the brink of calling for help, which would have disqualified Bryce, his eyes fell on Mark, standing on the shore. Cloud recounts what followed:

Mark gave him a huge fist pump and a yell, signaling to Bryce that he could do it. Their eyes locked for a few seconds, and, as Bryce described it, something happened—something beyond him. His body jumped into another gear, into another dimension of performance that he had not had access to before; he was able to get back on top of the cold water again and swim toward the finish line. He made it. He finished. He would be a SEAL.

That is the "power of the other."[1]

The church of Christ, comprised of His mighty Christian soldiers, should be a mutually encouraging people. Sir Fred Catherwood, British statesman and son-in-law of D. Martyn Lloyd-Jones, has rightly said, "The church should be the community of encouragement."[2] Paul wrote "to the church of the Thessalonians" (1 Thess. 1:1), "Therefore comfort [encourage, Greek *parakaleo*] one another with these words" (4:18), and "comfort [*parakaleo*] each other and edify one another, just as you also are doing" (5:11). He also writes, "We urge you, brethren, to recognize those who labor among you, and are over you in the Lord and admonish you" (5:12), and "We exhort you, brethren, warn those who are unruly, comfort the fainthearted, uphold the weak, be patient with all" (5:14).

What happened to Bryce, the tested-to-the-brink, wall-hitting, sinking wannabe Navy SEAL should constantly happen to out-of-fuel, straining, sinking siblings in Christ. When we sense that the lights are going out in a fellow believer's heart, we should supply eye-locking, fist-pumping encouragement to one another as we stand by as so "great a cloud of witnesses" (Heb. 12:1) to each other's epic swim home. Encouragement gives a shot of adrenaline.

---

1. Henry Cloud, *The Power of the Other: The Startling Effect Other People Have on You, from the Boardroom to the Bedroom and Beyond—And What to Do about It* (New York: Harper Business, 2016), 4–5.

2. As quoted in Rae Mackenzie, "Encourage One Another," blog of Lossie-mouth Baptist Church, January 30, 2016, https://lossiebaptist.org/encourage-one -another/.

Henry Cloud considers why a look and a fist pump from a friend were able to push Bryce beyond his physical and mental limits. He explains that the answer is mysterious:

> For centuries, philosophers, psychologists, theologians, and spiritual thinkers have struggled with something called the mind-body problem, the fact that the invisible has a real effect on the visible, and vice versa. But however we explain these mechanisms, the neglected truth is that the invisible attributes of relationship, the connection between people, have real, tangible, and measurable power....
>
> Relationship affects our physical and mental functioning throughout life. This invisible power, the power of the other, builds both the hardware and the software that leads to healthy functioning and better performance. For example, research shows over and over again that people trying to reach goals succeed at a much greater rate if they are connected to a strong human support system. Similarly, research shows that elderly people who have suffered heart attacks or strokes fare much better, with lower incidence of recurrence, when they join a support group. Other research has shown that people who tap into the power of the other have stronger immune systems, tend to get sick less frequently, and recover faster when they do.
>
> We can wonder how it happens and why, and strive to figure it out. But we can no longer dispute that it does happen. Relationship affects life and performance, period.[3]

In the church, we should daily seek to therapeutically empower one another.

Be a Barnabas Encourager

We've already met Barnabas in chapter 3, where we recounted how he wonderfully received Saul, the former persecutor of the church, and helped him to be graciously and properly recognized as Paul,

---

3. Cloud, *Power of the Other*, 6–7.

the apostle of the church (Acts 9). Earlier in Acts, we learn how Barnabas earned his name: "Joses, who was also named Barnabas by the apostles (which is translated Son of Encouragement), a Levite of the country of Cyprus, having land, sold it, and brought the money and laid it at the apostles' feet" (4:36–37).

This was a special, generous, and big-hearted man to be nicknamed Son of Encouragement by the Jerusalem apostles. And when there was news that revival had broken out far north in Antioch, the Jerusalem leaders tapped Barnabas as the one to send for the church-planting mission (Acts 11:22). Notice that they chose an encourager and not a nitpicker—a gracious and broad-minded Hellenist man born in Cyprus, and not a narrow-minded, circumcision-party Jerusalemite. This personality package was crucial for ministering to the Antioch Gentile culture, which was full of countless wild and woolly behavioral irregularities. Antioch was a questionable barbarian outpost in the eyes of tradition-entrenched Christian Jews.

Barnabas "was a good man, full of the Holy Spirit and of faith" (Acts 11:24). Good signifies more than mere moral worth; it means that he was a kind, genial, loving man. Many men—good, morally speaking—are stiff and hard. But Barnabas was a man of a gracious disposition—a very attractive man. A rash, haughty, domineering man, being critical of a church to which he was a stranger, would do more harm than good. But Barnabas, a son of sweetness and delight, would disarm opposition and secure confidence."[4] This is a mark of being "full of the Holy Spirit."

Barnabas went to Antioch to be a fact finder, not a faultfinder. Imagine the breathtaking pagan grave clothes of Daphne worship many of the Antiochene Gentile new converts probably were still wearing! But he was an optimistic man. This Son of Encouragement mind-set is a lesson to us all in the church. William Jay comments, "When all things are fair in character, you're not to go

---

4. J. Cynddylan Jones, commentary on Acts 11, in *Biblical Illustrator*, ed. Joseph S. Exell, https://www.studylight.org/commentaries/tbi/acts-11.html.

motive hunting. It is better to be occasionally deceived, than to live always in a temperature of suspicion. Divine grace is compatible with infirmities; otherwise we would exclude all from the possession of it. Our Savior does not despise 'the day of small things.' Let's follow His example."[5] These are insightful thoughts to consider when we deal with the wild and woolly youth and new converts in any church.

In the case of the youth, many say that they leave the church because other people are judgmental. Surely the church shouldn't take its moral cues from its youth and must not shrink back from pointing out sin. But too often we mistake sin for mere preference. David Murray wisely recognizes that "what many of these young people identify, however, is that the church seems at times to be *only* about judgment, *only* about critique, *only* about condemnation."[6] The apostle Paul writes in contrast to this, "Love suffers long and is kind…is not provoked…bears all things, believes all things, hopes all things" (1 Cor. 13:4–7).

When Barnabas "came and had seen the grace of God, he was glad, and encouraged them all that with purpose of heart they should continue with the Lord" (Acts 11:23). He beheld new and untaught Christians, viewed them as diamonds in the rough, and tactfully polished them with nonabrasive care.

This Barnabas is the same encourager who later "hoped all things" regarding John Mark, who had previously been a homesick quitter during Paul's first missionary journey: "John, departing from them, returned to Jerusalem" (Acts 13:13). But that wasn't the end of the John Mark story:

> Then after some days Paul said to Barnabas, "Let us now go back and visit our brethren in every city where we have preached the word of the Lord, and see how they are doing." Now Barnabas was determined to take with them John called

---

5. William Jay, commentary on Acts 11, in *Biblical Illustrator*, ed. Joseph S. Exell, http://biblehub.com/commentaries/illustrator/acts/11.htm.

6. Murray, *Happy Christian*, 129.

Mark. But Paul insisted that they should not take with them the one who had departed from them in Pamphylia, and had not gone with them to the work. Then the contention became so sharp that they parted from one another. And so Barnabas took Mark and sailed to Cyprus. (Acts 15:36–39)

Barnabas's magnanimous spirit paid off in a big way, as even Paul later admitted John Mark's great usefulness: "Get Mark and bring him with you, for he is useful to me for ministry" (2 Tim. 4:11).

I still remember over a decade ago when our firstborn was in college and was spiritually drowning. His hair looked long and wild and woolly to us. He was dating a young lady of questionable spirituality about whom Dad and Mom had warned. He was growing distant. Then out of nowhere, she broke up with him. He was devastated, brokenhearted, weeping, and emotionally sinking. And a "Barnabas" deacon in our church got in his car, drove to the far-away campus, put his arm around the boy, told him he loved him, reminded him of the Lord's goodness, handed him a modest fistful of cash, and drove away. That Barnabas "fist pump" of encouragement got my boy's head above water again. Priceless!

Be a Philemon or Onesiphorus Refresher

Philemon was a friend of Paul's at Colossae. Not only had Paul received hospitality from Philemon but the entire church met in his comfortable home. Paul wrote to Philemon, whom he called "our beloved friend and fellow laborer":

> I thank my God, making mention of you always in my prayers, hearing of your love and faith which you have toward the Lord Jesus and toward all the saints, that the sharing of your faith may become effective by the acknowledgment of every good thing which is in you in Christ Jesus. For we have great joy and consolation in your love, because the hearts of the saints have been refreshed by you, brother. (Philem. 2, 4–7)

Here Paul encourages a man known for being an encourager! What an uplifting commendation: "the hearts of the saints have been refreshed by you." It seems Philemon was like an iced lemonade on a hot summer day, a refreshment to his Christian brothers and sisters. But that's not always the case in the church. Sometimes we can have a suffocating influence on one another. Sam Crabtree writes, "Encouragement stands in contrast with the bent of human nature: grumbling, murmuring, complaining, fault-finding. Unfortunately there is a lot of cynicism in the church, as well as members thanklessly taking the goodness of others for granted, without stopping to comment with appreciation. Everyone's a critic. As a result, churches, marriages, and families can so easily become known for trying to win arguments more than trying to win hearts."[7]

Paul writes to seek a favor regarding Philemon's runaway, delinquent slave Onesimus, who needs Philemon's pardon and grace instead of justice and punishment. Paul trusts that, true to form, Philemon won't make him sweat: "Yes, brother, let me have joy from you in the Lord; refresh my heart in the Lord" (v. 20). Like Philemon, Onesiphorus was a church "refresher": "The Lord grant mercy to the household of Onesiphorus, for he often refreshed me, and was not ashamed of my chain" (2 Tim. 1:16).

It is a great pleasure to meet a twenty-first-century Philemon or Onesiphorus who refreshes suffocating saints. Jason Helopolous, a pastor at University Reformed Church in Lansing, Michigan, writes, "It has been my pleasure to serve in the local church with some individuals that are truly 'refreshing' to the saints. When you meet them, you know it! They are like an oasis in the midst of a desert. I walk away feeling encouraged, joyful, and spiritually stimulated. Unfortunately, they are an endangered species and much harder to find than should be the case."[8]

---

7. Sam Crabtree, "How to Cultivate Encouragement in Your Church," February 19, 2014, The Gospel Coalition, https://www.thegospelcoalition.org/article/how-to-cultivate-encouragement-in-your-church/.

8. Jason Helopolous, "20 Ways to Be Refreshing in the Local Church," October 16, 2014, *Restless and Reformed* (blog), The Gospel Coalition, https://www.thegospelcoalition.org/blogs/kevin-deyoung/20-ways-to-be-refreshing-in-the-local-church/.

Helopolous provides a list of practical ways we can be encouraging refreshers in our churches:

- Greet people on Sunday mornings with a smile. Go out of your way to say hello, ask questions about the lives of others, and listen attentively.

- Have a mouth overflowing with grace, and avoid speaking a "corrupt word" (Eph. 4:29).

- Show up each Sunday morning with a mental list of three or four people that you are going to find and minister to (Phil. 2:4). Many of us walk into church with an attitude of who will minister to us.

- Be a Monday morning encourager instead of a Monday morning critic by sending your pastor an appreciative email or note.

- Don't rush out of church on Sunday mornings. Be one of the last to leave.

- Routinely have a slow cooker meal or roast on Sundays and spontaneously invite over a visiting family or family in need after the service.

- Make visitors feel at home by greeting them and introducing them to others.

- Aim to remember peoples' names and greet them by name each Sunday.

- Refuse to speak badly of others in the congregation (Eph. 4:31).

- Speak with the children of the congregation (Matt. 19:14).

- Send notes of encouragement to members of the congregation anonymously.

- Seek to meet the needs of others in the congregation— spiritual, emotional, and financial—so that you are bearing others' burdens (Gal. 6:2). Be quick to forgive.

- Rejoice in the Lord (Phil. 4:4). Don't be an agitator or complainer.[9]

A refresher draws people to him or her like an air-conditioned lobby pulls overheated people from a blistering sidewalk. These kinds of encouraging behaviors create a refreshing atmosphere that promotes personal thriving and spiritual flourishing. Let's imitate Philemon and Onesiphorus.

Be a Tabitha Beautifier

Sam Crabtree describes a telling experience in a pastoral staff meeting when the staff was considering yet another email from a woman of the congregation known for her criticism and negativity: "In momentary silence while we pondered our options, one of the pastors spoke up: 'She is sure talented at spotting ways in which our church could improve.' At first we chuckled at his positivity; secretly, we all admired him for having such an uplifting attitude. We all needed more sanctification, and he saw this woman as a God-sent opportunity for that."[10]

Being known as a fault-finding nag in the church and among its members isn't a good thing. My wife, after kindly and tenderly showing love to a feeble and needy saint in our church body, reflected, "The older I get, the more I'm convinced that people don't need my confronting and criticizing, but my commending and encouraging!"

Tina recently joined our church. She has been a windfall to us. A few weeks ago at church, I was speaking with a dear brother, Doug, whose life is plagued with MS and its strangling squeeze on his health. The downbeat tone of our conversation indicated that he was spiritually gasping for breath and going under. And up walked Tina. I introduced her to Doug, whom she said she hadn't yet met. I told her Doug is the voice of an occasional timely "amen"

---

9. Helopolous, "20 Ways to Be Refreshing in the Local Church."
10. Crabtree, "How to Cultivate Encouragement in Your Church."

during some sermons. Her eyes brightened and she blurted out, "Oh, you're the one, Doug! I'm so thankful for your voice. It really enlivens the preaching for me!" She had no idea, but that comment was a huge boost that popped Doug back above water. Tina reminds me of Tabitha from Joppa, whose brief story is told in Acts 9:36–39:

> This woman was full of good works and charitable deeds which she did. But it happened in those days that she became sick and died. When they had washed her, they laid her in an upper room. And since Lydda was near Joppa, and the disciples had heard that Peter was there, they sent two men to him, imploring him not to delay in coming to them. Then Peter arose and went with them. When he had come, they brought him to the upper room. And all the widows stood by him weeping, showing the tunics and garments which Dorcas had made while she was with them.

Tabitha was a windfall to the Joppa church body, not troubling others with frowns of bitterness but adorning them with her charitable kindness. And the thought of losing her made everyone sick and desperate to get her back. That is the kind of an encouraging person everyone in the church should aspire to be.

Kimberly Wagner helps us in contrasting the destructively fierce Tabitha and the beautifully fierce Tabitha. Here is a sampling:

Destructively Fierce

1. She goes to battle often, mistaking her belligerence for heroism.

2. She grabs for power and no one and nothing prevents her from getting her way.

3. She uses her strength to bully others. Her continual criticisms, negative perspectives, and harsh tones are like acid.

4. She's harsh and blunt in her honesty and proud of it.

5. She is often involved in conflicts with others.

6. Her Bible study is merely academic; it doesn't affect how she treats others.

7. She usually has no trouble confronting, but her motive is for personal gain or comfort, and her approach is demeaning.

8. She walks in arrogance and pride but is blind to her lack of humility. She views meek behavior as a sign of weakness. She sincerely believes her personal conflicts stem from others' ineptness, lack of spirituality, or inferior behavior.

9. She craves power over others and has mastered the art of controlling them through subtle manipulation.

10. Although she may not admit it, her life is devoted to selfish pursuit. She's only satisfied when she gets her own way; she's unhappy with anything less.

Beautifully Fierce

1. Her identity and value are rooted in her relationship with Christ rather than a relationship with a man.

2. She's filled with gratitude for God's good gifts. Her heart is ruled by the peace of contentment.

3. She loves God and others. She's more focused on giving love than getting love.

4. She protects and defends the helpless rather than using her strength to bully others. She is known as a sincere encourager....

5. She has the power to influence and inspire because she lives under the Spirit's control....

6. Her life is lived all out for God's glory rather than the smallness of self....

7. She's honest but kind....

8. Others feel comfortable in seeking her counsel....

9. She embraces God's Word as her ultimate authority rather than being swayed by the voices of the culture....

10. She faithfully confronts by speaking truth in love rather than enabling sin by keeping silent.[11]

---

11. Kimberly Wagner, "The Fierce Women: Beautiful vs. Destructive," *Kimberly Wagner* (blog), September 26, 2012, https://www.kimberlywagner.org/2012/09/26/fierce-woman-characteristics/.

11

The Church and Strategic
ENCOURAGEMENT

There are times to scold. But 80 to 90 percent of what you
hope to correct can be accomplished through encouragement.

—Mark Dever

Paul Washer is anything but an ego-stroking motivational speaker. He is a straight-talking preacher of God's Word. But in a recorded 2017 sermon, he tells of having recently listened to a famous and notoriously misguided motivational speaker:

> I was very convicted. Just let that sink in for a moment [audience laughter]. I do believe that the things he was saying were out of context and wrong.... Where I was greatly rebuked was this. He was greatly encouraging with all his heart.... But I asked myself, "How encouraging am I?" [I thought about] how it is such a blessing when someone comes up to me and encourages me, and says, "Man, you're doing well. Man that was great, you're progressing." How it just jump-starts me, and I've found out it just jump-starts everyone else.... I just don't think by and large as God's people, at least for myself, I don't do that enough. "Wow, brother, sister, that was amazing. I'm so proud of God's grace in you. Keep going. Press on. Go on."[1]

As we saw in the last chapter, encouragement in the church is therapeutic in that it creates a healthy climate in which saints can

---

1. Paul Washer, "Walking with God" (sermon), July 2, 2017, https://www.sermonaudio.com/sermoninfo.asp?SID=72181529407.

spiritually thrive amid mutual encouragement. In this chapter, we'll see that encouragement in the church is also strategic in that it effectively jump-starts saints on to God-glorifying excellence in corporate endeavors.

Be a Proverbs 15 Evaluator

I talked once with a pastor of a large, pace-setting, gospel-preaching, Reformed, mature church. He admitted to me a significant weak spot in his elders' leadership: the mutual critiquing of one another's public sermons was nonexistent. Straight talk and mutually critical comments about personal preaching seemed to be too painful an experience to bear. Apparently, the elders feared that candid criticism might drive interpersonal wedges between them, so they just avoided evaluation altogether.

In contrast, the lead pastor of a large church I had the opportunity to visit invited me to attend a Sunday-evening elder/leadership forum that dissected every dimension of the day's ministry—from the delivery of each adult Sunday school lesson to the worship leader's welcoming salutation; the hymn selections; the congregation's singing; the music team's direction; the content and chemistry of the congregational prayer; the oral expression and commentary during the Scripture reading; and the content, length, and delivery of the sermon. There were about twenty-five men in the pastor's study, seated on sofas, love seats, stools, and folding chairs. Sitting there as an observer, I cringed when man after man stood naked and bare for open-season critical commentary on his performance earlier in the day, including some of the following observations:

- Your Sunday school outline was a bit logically disjointed.

- When you welcomed the congregation, you could have fully turned your body and visually scanned all of the seats and galleries.

- I thought the pace of that second hymn dragged a bit.

- It seemed a little awkward when you fell into that Puritan terminology when you prayerfully confessed the congregation's sin.

- Your reading tone sounded a bit mechanical during that poetic section.

- I know I sound like a broken record, Pastor, but I think sixty-five minutes is a little too long, and that you could have trimmed down some of the content and been even more effective.

I was struck with how deliberate this session was, how useful it was, and how different this leadership was from the elders who never engaged in critical evaluation for fear of offending and separating close friends. What a grand loss of opportunity there! What a windfall of benefit here!

But I also noticed that the ingredient that made it all work was encouragement. In every case of commentary in the study that night, words of encouragement were enlisted to brighten the eyes of the patient on the X-ray table. It is obvious that plenty of instruction and discipline had gone into deliberately training this leadership team on how to wisely sharpen each other's iron for genuine benefit.

- Your illustration on how a husband can calm a wife's irritation was golden. You had everyone smiling but thinking!

- You came across really warm when you personally recognized Mrs. Brown's return to the congregation after so many weeks of sickness.

- Whoever selected that fourth hymn was brilliant. Fit perfectly as a lead-in to the sermon, and singing the final verse a capella made my hair stand up on the back of my neck.

- I thought your confessing the sin of our viewing children as an interfering lifestyle nuisance was so helpful in alerting our young couples to the danger of self-indulgence in marriage.

- You perfectly set up the entire Scripture reading by that pithy quote from Mathew Henry's commentary.

- You could have heard a pin drop, Pastor, when you pointed out the self-idolatry of picking seats of honor at the table. It hit me right between the eyes.

Encouragement was the lidocaine numbing and freezing the area for the critical and medicinal needle that followed or preceded. The whole session, which closed around 11 p.m., was a showcase of Proverbs 15 wisdom:

> A soft answer turns away wrath,
> But a harsh word stirs up anger.
> The tongue of the wise uses knowledge rightly,
> But the mouth of fools pours forth foolishness....

> A wholesome [soothing, NASB; gentle, ESV]
>   tongue is a tree of life,
> But perverseness in it breaks the spirit....

> The lips of the wise disperse knowledge,
> But the heart of the fool does not do so.

> A scoffer does not love one who corrects him,
> Nor will he go to the wise.

> The heart of him who has understanding
>   seeks knowledge,
> But the mouth of fools feeds on foolishness.

> A wrathful man stirs up strife,
> But he who is slow to anger allays contention.

> Without counsel, plans go awry,
> But in the multitude of counselors they are established.

> A man has joy by the answer of his mouth,
> And a word spoken in due season, how good it is!

> The thoughts of the wicked are an abomination to
>   the LORD,
> But the words of the pure are pleasant.

The heart of the righteous studies how to answer,
But the mouth of the wicked pours forth evil.
The light of the eyes rejoices the heart,
And a good report makes the bones healthy.
The ear that hears the rebukes of life
Will abide among the wise.
He who disdains instruction despises his own soul,
But he who heeds rebuke gets understanding.
The fear of the LORD is the instruction of wisdom,
And before honor is humility.
(vv. 1–2, 4, 7, 12, 14, 18, 22–23, 26, 28, 30–33)

It is true that the hard-hitting style of this large church may be too much for more interpersonally sensitive eldership and leadership teams. And it is possible that indiscreet comments can be spoken, that less-than-noble personal agendas can be sounded, and that damaging offenses can be absorbed. Doing good involves taking risks. And not all churches have to analyze their services as this one did. But also keep in mind the wonderful, multidimensional, strategic capabilities of well-crafted encouragement. You can almost painlessly criticize by offering creative and sincere praise.

A very gifted seminarian has occasionally filled the pulpit in our church. His expositions and explanations of passages are accurate and sound, but he tends to be satisfied with making objective declarations without employing enlightening illustrations. His preaching comes across at times a little bland. Not knowing him well and having little personal capital with him, I expressed sincere appreciation for his exegetical precision and carefulness in handling the text after his first couple of sermons. But the third time, he used an illustration from World War II and applied it to a Christian's warfare against the world, the flesh, and the devil. It provided traction, woke up the congregation, and gripped our attention. After the sermon I told him so, expressing that he really "had us" during that moment, and I encouraged him to sprinkle every sermon with the seasoning of well-timed pictures.

The wise and sincere use of encouragement is a strategic tool in the church for the building up of the saints to make us better servants of our King.

Be an Appreciative Member

I know that pastors can be very foolish, sinful, negligent, and worthy of much legitimate criticism—and even discipline. But this is a book about encouragement. Pastors can also be wise, sincere, diligent, and worthy of much esteem and appreciation: "And we urge you, brethren, to recognize [appreciate, NASB; respect, ESV] those who labor among you, and are over you in the Lord and admonish you, and to esteem them very highly in love for their work's sake. Be at peace among yourselves" (1 Thess. 5:12–13).

This is true, even though every pastor is riddled with weakness and the infirmity of clay feet. But Paul reminds us of the reason for our weakness: "We have this treasure in earthen vessels, that the excellence of the power may be of God and not of us" (2 Cor. 4:7).

Consider this anonymously told folktale:

An elderly Chinese woman had two large pots, each hung on the ends of a pole which she carried across her neck. One of the pots had a crack in it while the other pot was perfect and always delivered a full portion of water. At the end of the long walks from the stream to the house, the cracked pot arrived only half full. For a full two years this went on daily, with the woman bringing home only one and a half pots of water. Of course, the perfect pot was proud of its accomplishments. But the poor cracked pot was ashamed of its own imperfection, and miserable that it could only do half of what it had been made to do. After two years of what it perceived to be bitter failure, it spoke to the woman one day by the stream. "I am ashamed of myself, because this crack in my side causes water to leak out all the way back to your house." The old woman smiled. "Did you notice that there are flowers on your side of the path, but not on the other pot's side? That's because I have always known about your flaw, so I planted flower seeds on your side of the path, and every day while we walk back, you water them. For two years I have been able to pick these beautiful flowers to decorate the table. Without you being just the way you are, there would not be this beauty to grace the house."

Each of us has our unique flaws. Like me, your pastor probably knows he is riddled with flaws and is a bit ashamed of his cracks. But typically it is many of those very deformities that the Lord uses to grow His church. Find ways to let him know you appreciate him. Kevin DeYoung's insight is helpful:

Here is one simple and very important thing you can do to encourage your pastor: tell him you are grateful for his preaching....

If your pastor's sermon helped you see more of Jesus, or helped you turn from sin, or helped you understand the Bible better, or helped you be a better spouse, or helped you trust God in the midst of suffering, or stirred your affections for the things of glory, tell him. It doesn't have to be every week or even every month. But when appropriate, and when legitimate, tell him. It can be as short as a two sentence email or a ten-second conversation at the door.... A little bit of encouragement will go a lot farther than you think....

I don't say this because pastors have the hardest job on the planet. In a lot of ways, it's the most privileged job on the planet. But being a pastor is unique in that every week our work—and really our heart and soul—is put on display for everyone to see, savor, or sleep through. It's natural that a pastor would wonder from time to time, "How am I doing?"

Most often, I don't think the question rattles around the pastor's head because of narcissism, low self-esteem, or selfish ambition. I think most pastors genuinely have no idea if they are making any difference in the lives of their people. I think ministers spend a lot of time quietly wondering if they are just whistling in the dark....

Don't worry about his head getting too big. The Lord knows how to keep his pastors humble so you can worry about keeping your pastor going....

"Whatever is true, whatever is honorable, whatever is just, whatever is pure, whatever is lovely, whatever is commendable, if there is any excellence, if there is anything worthy of praise, thinking about these things" (Phil. 3:8). And if your pastor's sermon—even once in a great while—falls into the category of "these things," give thanks to God. And consider letting your pastor know that you did.[2]

Be a Boaz Pastor

Many years ago Doug, the man in our church with MS, came to me and suggested we add a word of benediction, a parting pastoral word of blessing from God to the congregation, to the end of our services. He said that while he worshiped for a couple of years at a Presbyterian church, he grew to value the pastoral blessings at the conclusion of the service. I admit that I was initially nonplussed. But eventually the weight of the Scriptures took its toll on me, and I saw the value of adding a benediction.

Think biblically with me. In Ruth 2, we meet Boaz, the great-grandfather of David. He made sure his household breathed the air of benediction, bestowing blessings on his workmen morning by morning:

> Now behold, Boaz came from Bethlehem, and said to the reapers, "The LORD be with you!"
> And they answered him, "The LORD bless you!" (v. 4)

I'd love to work for a man like that! Who wouldn't want to live in Boaz's household?

God's household ought to have an air of blessing more than an air of demanding or criticizing. And pastors ought to set that kind

---

2. Kevin DeYoung, "One Simple Way to Encourage Your Pastor," July 28, 2015, *Restless and Reformed* (blog), The Gospel Coalition, https://www.thegospelcoalition .org/right_now_link/one-simple-way-to-encourage-your-pastor/.

of encouraging tone. Consider the writer of Hebrews. In the finale of his hard-hitting letter, seasoned with multiple warning sections, he bids farewell to his endangered and beloved flock with what is considered the Mount Everest of the New Testament benedictions: "Now may the God of peace who brought up our Lord Jesus from the dead, that great Shepherd of the sheep, through the blood of the everlasting covenant, make you complete in every good work to do His will, working in you what is well pleasing in His sight, through Jesus Christ, to whom be glory forever and ever. Amen" (Heb. 13:20–21). What encouragement this was to this little church in Rome, harassed with persecution, probably in the crosshairs of mad Emperor Nero's wrath!

Words have power. One man confided to his pastor, "My dad always told me I'd never amount to anything, and I believed it." Like a curse, those cruel fatherly words weakened and crippled the son. Likewise, gracious fatherly words, a blessing, strengthen and embolden a son. On His way to face His Jerusalem execution, Jesus basked in His Father's benediction smile on the Mount of Transfiguration:

> Now after six days Jesus took Peter, James, and John his brother, led them up on a high mountain by themselves; and He was transfigured before them. His face shone like the sun, and His clothes became as white as the light....
>
> While he was still speaking, behold, a bright cloud overshadowed them; and suddenly a voice came out of the cloud, saying, "This is My beloved Son, in whom I am well pleased. Hear Him!" (Matt. 17:1–2, 5)

The Son of God was braced and bolstered by benediction blessing, and so are all the sons of God. Likewise the Hebrews writer beams: "the God of peace." This is such a warm title for God in the ears of hell-deserving traitors whose sins would sentence them to gnash their teeth forever in outer darkness. That is because "while [they] were still sinners, Christ died for" them (Rom. 5:8), because while they were yet "enemies" they "were reconciled to God through the death of His Son" (5:10).

He continues beaming: "through the blood of the everlasting covenant"—they were not just pardoned by a grandfatherly wink, but by a bloody sacrifice. Sinclair Ferguson talks about the old Scottish tradition of reporting the public execution of a convicted murderer in a newspaper headline that would read, "John McMillan was justified yesterday at noon, at his hanging." This meant that the criminal was made right with Scotland, having paid off justice at the price of his own life. Christ's blood wrote in bright red "paid in full" over every believer's debt ledger. God spared not His own Son (Rom. 8:32). So we are no longer disgusting criminals in His eyes, but adorable children, freshly washed and wrapped in a thick bath towel.

He beams on: "the God of peace who brought up our Lord Jesus from the dead, that great Shepherd of the sheep." The Lord Jesus now ever lives to intercede for us, and comforts us in dark valleys with His goodness and mercy (see Ps. 23:6).

Finally, the Hebrews writer beams: "make you complete in every good work to do His will." We are no longer spiritual villains but have been re-created into kingdom mighty men and women armed with spiritual weaponry (see Eph. 6:13–18), able to fight the good fight of faith (see 1 Tim. 6:12).

The Hebrews writer sends the army of the saints out of the church barracks with this rousing benediction and conviction that, as Paul says, "we are more than conquerors through Him who loved us" (Rom. 8:37). Remember who you are, church! Nothing "shall be able to separate [you] from the love of God which is in Christ Jesus our Lord" (v. 39). That is the encouraging kind of atmosphere that a new covenant pastor should create for the children of God assigned to his care. And creating this climate of encouragement goes far beyond just giving a liturgical benediction at the end of services. It is having an overall tone that shapes your ministry.

In chapter 9 I wrote about the danger for fathers of falling into a rut of chronically reprimanding and badgering their children.

Skim over that section again and ponder. Pastors can fall into that same rut with their congregations. They can unwittingly take on as a habit the scorching pitch of a prosecuting attorney, addressing primarily guilty criminals, instead of the encouraging tone of a loving pastor shepherding halting sheep. Surely stern gusts of warning and reproof are essential for faithful pastoring and persevering, but that is not to be the prevailing wind. With a steady diet of criticism, people wither up. But with prevailing encouragement, they get encouraged.

Mark Dever expressed it this way in his book *Discipling: How to Help Others Follow Jesus*: "So many times I've seen men, particularly younger guys, act as if real leadership is shown in correcting others. That's why young men's sermons often scold. What they haven't figured out is that you can often accomplish more by encouragement. There are times to scold. But 80 to 90 percent of what you hope to correct can be accomplished through encouragement. If you look back at your life and consider who influenced you the most, you will probably find it's the people who believed in you."[3]

Encouragement and benediction should be the prevailing wind and breath of our pastoral ministries to the church of Christ. I think that is what battle-worn Doug instinctively and legitimately craves from me and my ministry—an overall climate of cheering benediction and blessing.

Be a Bruised-Reed Consoler

Sometimes we think that the best way we can encourage struggling brothers and sisters is to present ourselves as spiritually strong and sturdy Washington Monuments. That way, we think, weak and fainting folks will be better able to lean on us. But often we are more effective when we transparently expose ourselves as fearing

---

3. Mark Dever, *Discipling: How to Help Others Follow Jesus*, 9 Marks: Building Healthy Churches (Wheaton, Ill.: Crossway, 2016), 101.

and trembling bruised reeds. That way, feeble souls, sensing our empathy, are better able to receive resuscitation from us.

In chapter 2, I mentioned the struggles of Philip Ryken, president of Wheaton College. He encouraged the entire student body during a September 2014 chapel message. Many of them were probably struggling themselves. Among his listeners most likely were freshmen dying on the inside of homesickness, sophomores feeling paralyzed by academic pressures, juniors sensing the burden of out-of-control student loans, and seniors fearful of not having a job, a romantic interest, or a plan by the time May rolled around. Titling his chapel message "Nobody Knows the Trouble I've Seen," Ryken explained that he had begun experiencing trouble the previous semester because someone he loved was troubled, fearful, sad, and thinking that life was not worth living. He prayed, asking God to lift her burden and allow him to carry it instead. In the ensuing weeks and months that followed, Ryken noticed that while his loved one's suffering was relieved, he was feeling overwhelming sadness:

> Truthfully many mornings I cried all the while I was getting ready for the day. I was struck with broken relationships, multiple attacks on my character, revisiting of painful experiences from the past. I'm not sure it was the best semester for me to go through my 360-degree performance review and get honest feedback about my leadership from faculty, alumni, and students. All of this made me very anxious. There were nights when I did not sleep well, which is rare for me. Many mornings I was up well before dawn. There were days when it was very hard to get up and face the day. I doubt I was very good company. I'm sad about that. My problems were consuming so much emotional energy that it was hard to be with people very many hours at a time. I just needed to go and be alone through the day.

When Ryken's wife convinced him to go to the doctor, he scored badly on a checklist for emotional health. He wondered if God loved him. Doubts and guilt crept in, leading him to wonder if he was even a Christian. He began to spiral downward and have suicidal thoughts, which he realizes were Satan's temptations. He was in real danger. But he concluded his account with these thoughts:

> But I want to tell you that God did not abandon me, but rescued me. My loving Lord Jesus Christ brought me safely through. I can't say my troubles are over. I can't say my feelings of despair will never return. But I know that my Lord will be "a present help in times of trouble" (Ps. 46:1).
>
> That's my testimony.[4]

Ryken went on to explain in detail how the Lord came to rescue his soul and how Jesus was a very present help in that dark time of trouble. And the effect of that sermon was like a shot of adrenaline to his audience. I know it was not only because I heard reports from witnesses but also because when I viewed the video of that sermon, my own heart was dramatically resuscitated in the middle of my own time of trouble.

Ryken's technique wasn't really anything new. He simply took a page out of the apostle Paul's ministry manual. Note that the italicized words are all translated from the Greek word *paraklesis*, which means "encouragement":

> Blessed be the God and Father of our Lord Jesus Christ, the Father of mercies and God of all *comfort*, who *comforts* us in all our tribulation, that we may be *able to comfort* those who are in any trouble, with the *comfort* with which we ourselves *are comforted* by God. For as the sufferings of Christ abound in us, so our *consolation* also abounds through Christ. Now if we are afflicted, it is for your *consolation* and salvation, which is effective for enduring the same sufferings which we also suffer. Or if we are *comforted*, it is for your *consolation* and salvation. And our hope for you is steadfast, because we know that as you are partakers of the sufferings, so also you will partake of the consolation.
>
> For we do not want you to be ignorant, brethren, of our trouble which came to us in Asia: that we were burdened

---

4. Ryken, "Nobody Knows the Trouble I've Seen."

beyond measure, above strength, so that we despaired even
of life. Yes, we had the sentence of death in ourselves, that we
should not trust in ourselves but in God who raises the dead.
(2 Cor. 1:3–9)

Paul didn't pretend to be an immovable monument. Instead,
he candidly confessed he was a bruised reed, susceptible to crushing burdens and withering winds. He survived, emotionally and
spiritually, only by the resuscitating help of Jesus, who nursed him
back from his depths of despair and times of trouble. This kind of
candid admission greatly encourages fellow bruised reeds.

Don't pretend to be something you're not. Imitate Paul. Divulge
your frailty. It will console other people and encourage the saints.

The employment of these strategic encouragement principles in church life—wise evaluating, appreciative commending,
benediction-toned pastoring, and bruised-reed consoling—
wonderfully jump-starts members to do great things for God. It is
like adrenaline.

12

The Companion of
ENCOURAGEMENT

Nothing can be more cruel than the leniency which aban-
dons others to their sin. Nothing can be more compassionate
than the severe reprimand which calls another Christian in
one's community back from the path of sin.
—Dietrich Bonhoeffer

In July 2017, Jordan Spieth, the precocious young PGA golf phe-
nomenon, held a slim lead entering the final round of the major,
prestigious Open Championship at Royal Birkdale in England. On
the first tee, Spieth had no idea what kind of an emotional roller
coaster run he was in for. It was Spieth's caddie, Michael Greller,
who kept him from collapsing. And it wasn't just by giving "sweet
kisses" of encouragement. Spieth's first-hole tee shot took a bad
bounce into a patch of tall grass. When the pair assessed the dam-
age, the television microphones picked up the player/caddie banter:

> Spieth: "That's just garbage man...to not get
> rewarded for a good shot!"
>
> Greller: "Alright! Get over it!"

Greller knows Spieth, who is typically the consummate gentle-
man. Sensing Spieth was at risk of slipping into an emotional pity
party early on, Greller delivered a well-timed reproof that arrested
the attitude slide. Instead of fawning and pampering Spieth by
treating him like a prima donna, Greller rebuked him, challeng-
ing him to man up. At the end of the day, Spieth was holding the

Claret Jug trophy in the winner's circle and was praising Greller for his mind-steadying guidance along the way.

Spurring on to excellence often involves loving criticism—that's the healthy companion of adrenalizing encouragement. I touched on this theme of criticism in chapter 7 when I addressed the concern about unduly pampering people. An entire book could be written about godly criticism, but since this is a book on encouragement, we'll just address it in one chapter.

The Spurring On of Criticism

In chapter 1, I wrote about Jerry Kramer, the All-Pro offensive guard of the Green Bay Packers, whose career was salvaged by the locker room adrenaline talk of his legendary coach Vince Lombardi. You may remember that Lombardi spied the disheartened Kramer on the verge of quitting, with his face in his hands, sitting on the bench in front of his locker. The eventual Hall of Fame coach sized up the situation, walked over, messed up Kramer's sweaty hair, and said, "Son, someday you're going to be one of the greatest guards in football." Those encouraging words were a timely shot of adrenaline that propelled Kramer into football stardom.

But I need to tell you the rest of the story because it is an important part that demonstrates Lombardi's greatness, according to Kramer. Earlier that same day, Kramer was having a bad time on the field. During a goal line scrimmage, he couldn't seem to do anything right. He was jumping offside, missing his assignments, and getting late to his blocks. Kramer tells what happened:

> Lombardi got right in my face. "Mister," he yelled, "the attention span of a grade school kid is 30 seconds, for a high school kid a minute, for a college kid three minutes. Mister, where does that leave you?" By the end of practice, I was ready to quit.[1]

---

1. Voight, *Sports Leadership Playbook*, 125.

And then we know what happened when Kramer was despondent in the locker room.

The hair-messing encouragement was preceded by the face-mask-grabbing criticism. In Lombardi's case, the companion of adrenalized encouragement was loving criticism. Kramer says about his late coach, "There was just something about him that brought out the best a man could give. He loved you enough to push you to be all you could be."[2]

In 1959, Lombardi arrived in Green Bay, facing a team that had a pathetic record of one win, ten losses, and one tie the previous year. By 1961, he coached the Packers into a championship; and between 1961 and 1967, the Packers won the championship five times, including three years in a row, a feat not matched since. Lombardi is the benchmark of football coaching excellence. The chief secret to success was his dogged determination to encourage his players to pursue excellence in everything they did on the football field. His view was that if the players would just do everything with excellence, they would get the crown. Lombardi said, "Perfection is not attainable, but if we chase perfection we can catch excellence."[3]

On a radio broadcast that featured Kramer, the host talked about the priceless blessing of having Lombardi-like people in our lives to push us to greatness. He asked his listeners to call in and share their personal stories. The first man to call said that for him, that person was an elementary school teacher who was a Roman Catholic nun. "I was a Spanish-speaking third grader who didn't know a lick of English, but she demanded that I be immersed in English, and pursue excellence in the endeavor. I'm now a writer for the *Wall Street Journal*. Without her Lombardi-like pushing, I'd never be where I am right now." Another caller spoke of her boss, who told her to stop feeling sorry for herself. Another told of his

2. Jerry Kramer, interview by Dennis Prager, *Dennis Prager Show*, February 2011.

3. Chuck Carlson, *Game of My Life: Memorable Stories of Packer Football* (Champaign, Ill.: Sports Publishing, 2004), 149.

demanding father, and another of his urging mother. Let's consider how the Bible is full of this spurring on to excellence.

The Writer of Hebrews

The writer of the book of Hebrews offers this encouragement: "And let us consider one another in order to stir up [stimulate, NASB] love and good works, not forsaking the assembling of ourselves together, as is the manner of some, but exhorting one another, and so much the more as you see the Day approaching" (10:24–25).

The writer enlists a strategic word to push his readers to be all they can be spiritually. Stir up (or stimulate) one another! It is the Greek word *paroxusmon*, which refers to a sharp disagreement (like when Paul and Barnabas differed sharply about John Mark's reliability in Acts 15:39). Its verb form, *paraxuno*, means "to provoke," or even "to upset." We speak of a *paroxysm*, a coughing fit, which seeks to stir up (upset) our lungs to rid them of excess phlegm. We irritatingly spur a horse. We agitatingly goad an ox. We sharpen an ax at a grindstone, creating sparks. In Acts 17:16 Paul was "provoked within" as he observed the city of Athens was "given over to idols." He was irritated to action. And so the writer to the Hebrews urges his readers to stimulate one another to love and good works.

This kind of strategic provoking works! Think of the young woman who sets sail on the pursuit of a four-year bachelor's degree in nursing (BSN). Her parents help, paying half the tuition. But after her junior year, she runs out of motivation, quits school, and gets marooned in a department store job. After patiently watching her daughter sit out a semester, Mom takes her aside and kindly, yet firmly expresses how deeply disappointed she and Dad are in her. She is burying God-given talent and opportunity. Stung by the criticism and feeling ashamed of herself, she uses the aroused passion to fuel her senior-year final stretch to her BSN.

A. W. Pink describes the intention of the writer to the Hebrews: "The chief design is to stir up performance, to strengthen zeal, to inflame affections, to excite unto godly living by godly example, by suitable exhortations, by unselfish acts of kindness. We are to fire one another unto love…never winking at sin…or shrinking back from warning or rebuking where such is necessary. We're not to ask how little we might do for Christ just to get by, but how much we might do to win His smile."[4] John Brown pens, "They are to act the part which is calculated to call forth in one another's bosoms the workings of that peculiar affection which all Christians have (to the Lord) and to each other."[5]

The story is told of Francis Marion, the legendary Swamp Fox patriot, whose guerrilla tactics against the British Redcoats helped turn the tide for the colonists during the Revolutionary War. At Yorktown, Marion was watching a wave of American forces retreating in the face of withering British cannon and rifle fire. He couldn't bear it. He grabbed a tattered American flag and ran head-long back into the teeth of the British guns, shouting at the top of his lungs, "Forward! Forward! Forward!" This indicting and spurring display of patriotic heroism reproved cowardice and inspired courage, resulting in a tide-turning charge that broke Britain's back.

That is how Christians are to spur one another on. They need to say, "Don't quit! Don't give up or be lethargic or indifferent or cowardly or lazy! Come on, fight the good fight. Rouse yourselves up! Charge forward for Christ and against sin! Brother! Sister! Our Savior is worthy of our wholehearted best! Excellence!"

The Proverbial Father

This dogged determination to be spurred on to spiritual excellence is throughout the Bible. God's Word pushes us. It doesn't pamper us. It spurs us on to excellence, to Christlikeness. It doesn't massage in mediocrity. It doesn't let us feel okay about our flabbiness or sloppiness.

---

4. A. W. Pink, *An Exposition of Hebrews* (Grand Rapids: Baker Books, 2003), 603.

5. John Brown, *Hebrews*, Geneva Series Commentary (London: Banner of Truth, 1972), 465.

Echoing the heavenly Father, the father in the book of Proverbs isn't content just to hang around the house as a nice person, simply warmly affirming his son's (and daughter's) mediocre game. He urges his son to strive to get to the next level. And he is not afraid to sound a negative note:

> My son, hear the instruction of your father,
> And do not forsake the law [teaching] of your mother;
> For they will be a graceful ornament on your head,
> And chains about your neck.
>
> My son, if sinners entice you,
> Do not consent. (1:8–10)
>
> My son, do not walk in the way with them,
> Keep your foot from their path. (1:15)
>
> My son, do not despise the chastening of the LORD,
> Nor detest His correction;
> For whom the LORD loves He corrects,
> Just as a father the son in whom he delights. (3:11–12)
>
> My son, give attention to my words;
> Incline your ear to my sayings.
> Do not let them depart from your eyes;
> Keep them in the midst of your heart;
> For they are life to those who find them,
> And health to all their flesh.
> Keep your heart with all diligence,
> For out of it spring the issues of life.
> Put away from you a deceitful mouth,
> And put perverse lips far from you.
> Let your eyes look straight ahead,
> And your eyelids look right before you.
> Ponder the path of your feet,
> And let all your ways be established.
> Do not turn to the right or the left;
> Remove your foot from evil. (4:20–27)

A fool despises his father's instruction,
But he who receives correction is prudent. (15:5)

This father sounds a bit like Vince Lombardi. He wants his son to pursue excellence. My dad was like this, so I know there is something inside that makes us wince at these urgings. Frankly, during the summers, I would sometimes be relieved to discover on my dad's days off that he was called in to work for overtime hours because it meant he wouldn't be making demands on me that day and I could just take it easy. On reflection, though, I'm overwhelmingly thankful for my dad's lifelong spurring, and when we are thinking correctly, we should all yearn for it.

Lucy Montgomery's *Anne of Green Gables* brilliantly unzips the human heart. In one chapter, the teenage orphan Anne Shirley, an aspiring author, tells Marilla, her adoptive guardian, that she no longer writes childishly as before, when she thought she was so profound: "Miss Stacy sometimes has us write a story for training purposes in composition, and she criticizes it very sharply and makes us criticize our own too. I never thought my compositions had so many faults until I began to look for them myself. I felt so ashamed I wanted to give up altogether, but Miss Stacy said I could learn to write well if I only trained myself to be my own severest critic. And so I am trying to."[6] In the insightful story, Anne absolutely reveled in learning under Miss Stacy. Eventually, because she worked so hard under Miss Stacy, she won the coveted Avery Scholarship for academic excellence.

I still remember that D+ I received from Mrs. VanHaitsma for my first college essay in creative writing. The pages were bleeding red ink that pointed out immaturity in my writing style. I had gotten a diet of As in high school. Mrs V. rocked my world and forced me to elevate my skills.

---

6. Lucy Maud Montgomery, *Anne of Green Gables* (New York: Grosset & Dunlap, 1908), 356.

Tim Keller, who says that his wife's verbal affirmation has in some ways made him into a "superman," gives a crucial balancing word, lest we fall into the error of neglecting verbal correction:

> Sometimes we let fly some (truthful but) real harsh, insulting remarks, and the next thing we know there's nothing left of our spouses but a pair of sneakers with smoke coming out of them.... When we see how devastating truth-telling in marriage can be, it can push us into the opposite error. We may then decide that our job is just to affirm. We avoid telling our spouses how disappointed we are. We shut up. We stuff and hide what we really think and feel. We exercise the power of love, but not the power of truth.
>
> But then marriage's enormous potential for spiritual growth is lost. If I come to realize that my spouse is not really being truthful with me, then her loving affirmations become less powerful in my life. Only when I know that my spouse regularly tells me the truth will her loving affirmations really change me.[7]

Supportive encouraging must be intertwined with truthful spurring. What football player who seeks championship rings and Hall of Fame accolades wouldn't want a Lombardi-like coach? What Christian who seeks "Well done, good and faithful servant" from his Lord Jesus wouldn't want a spurring pastor, spouse, or friend?

The Apostle Paul

Notice how Paul combines rather blunt exhortations with affectionate encouragement in pushing his beloved brothers and sisters to a higher standard of excellence:

> Do you not know that those who run in a race all run, but one receives the prize? Run in such a way that you may obtain it. And everyone who competes for the prize is temperate in all things. Now they do it to obtain a perishable crown, but

---

7. Keller and Keller, *Meaning of Marriage*, 162–63.

we for an imperishable crown. Therefore I run thus: not with uncertainty. Thus I fight: not as one who beats the air. But I discipline my body and bring it into subjection, lest, when I have preached to others, I myself should become disqualified. (1 Cor. 9:24–27)

Watch, stand fast in the faith, be brave [literally, "act like men"], be strong. (1 Cor. 16:13)

Therefore, having these promises, beloved, let us cleanse ourselves from all filthiness of the flesh and spirit, perfecting holiness in the fear of God. (2 Cor. 7:1)

Not that I have already attained, or am already perfected; but I press on, that I may lay hold of that for which Christ Jesus has also laid hold of me. Brethren, I do not count myself to have apprehended; but one thing I do, forgetting those things which are behind and reaching forward to those things which are ahead, I press toward the goal for the prize of the upward call of God in Christ Jesus. (Phil. 3:12–14)

But we were gentle among you, just as a nursing mother cherishes her own children. So, affectionately longing for you, we were well pleased to impart to you not only the gospel of God, but also our own lives, because you had become dear to us. For you remember, brethren, our labor and toil; for laboring night and day, that we might not be a burden to any of you....

As you know how we exhorted, and comforted, and charged every one of you, as a father does his own children, that you would walk worthy of God who calls you into His own kingdom and glory. (1 Thess. 2:7–12)

Notice how tender motherly nurturing was flanked by Lombardi-like fatherly spurring. Neither Vince Lombardi nor the apostle Paul pampered their players.

In 1969, Nathaniel Branden's trendsetting publication *The Psychology of Self-Esteem* claimed that self-esteem was the single most important facet of a person. Since then, the belief that people must do whatever they can to achieve positive self-esteem has become a movement with broad societal effects. Anything potentially damaging to children's self-esteem has been done away with. Competitions are frowned on. Soccer coaches have stopped counting goals and hand out trophies to everyone. Teachers have thrown out their red pencils. Criticism has been replaced with ubiquitous and even undeserved praise.[8]

The apostle Paul obviously never got that memo: "Do you not know that those who run in a race all run, but one receives the prize? Run in such a way that you may obtain it [win, NASB]" (1 Cor. 9:24). Paul knew that "trophies for everyone" doesn't work. People must strive aggressively for worthwhile prizes, and research is proving it. In 2003 Dr. Roy Baumeister, then a leading proponent of self-esteem, conducted a rigorous study that he humorously reported "was the biggest disappointment of my career." His team concluded that the self-esteem movement was undeniably polluted with flawed science.[9]

In 2007, Lisa Blackwell conducted research between a control group and a test group of math students. The test group was given two twenty-five-minute sessions teaching them a single idea, that the brain is a muscle, and giving it a harder workout makes you smarter. The control group didn't attend the "brain is a muscle" sessions. It didn't take long. The teachers—who hadn't known which students had been given the sessions—could pick out the students who had been taught that intelligence can be developed. The test group students improved their study habits and grades. In a single semester, Blackwell reversed the students' longtime trend of

---

8. Po Bronson, "How Not to Talk to Your Kids,"*New York Magazine*, August 3, 2007, http://nymag.com/news/features/27840/index2.html.

9. Roy F. Baumeister et al., "Does High Self-Esteem Cause Better Performance, Interpersonal Success, Happiness, or Healthier Lifestyles?," *Psychological Science in the Public Interest* 4, no. 1 (May 2003): 1–44, https://www.ncbi.nlm.nih.gov/pubmed/26151640.

decreasing math grades.[10] That finding echoes Paul's spurring conviction regarding the pursuit of excellence.

The Lord Jesus

Notice the tactful strategy of the Master Good Shepherd in guiding and urging His precious flock homeward. He wasn't laid back and easygoing. He was tender *and* tough.

Todd Schenck is a shepherd of sorts. He was the cross country coach for a high school team that was a rival to my children's. I always admired Schenck's coaching style. He would run around the 3.1 mile course with a rustic shepherd's staff in hand, shouting verbal spurs at his runners. He would tell them that they looked great, that he needed them to dig deep, that the team was counting on them to move up and score crucial points. When one of his runners approached that heartbreak hill for which the course was notoriously known, Schenck would trumpet, "Bull up! Bull up!" And when the spent runner crested the peak, Schenck would bellow, "Bird down! Bird down!" More than once, his teams took the state title. He provided life-defining experiences for his runners.

Jesus is the best at boldly pushing us on to excellence. He spurs us on to win the only trophy really worth having. In the Olivet Discourse he trumpets urgency in His parable of the talents by heartily commending the good servants and severely reprimanding the bad servant (see Matt. 25:19–26, 30). To the responsible two-talent and five-talent slaves, he commended: "Well done, good and faithful servant…. Enter into the joy of your lord." But to the irresponsible one-talent slave, he reprimanded, "You wicked and lazy servant… and cast the unprofitable servant into the outer darkness."

In the garden of Gethsemane He sounds the waking bugle of reveille:

He took Peter, James, and John with Him, and He began to be troubled and deeply distressed. Then He said to them, "My

---

10. Bronson, "How Not to Talk to Your Kids."

soul is exceedingly sorrowful, even to death. Stay here and watch."....

Then He came and found them sleeping, and said to Peter, "Simon, are you sleeping? Could you not watch one hour? Watch and pray, lest you enter into temptation. The spirit indeed is willing, but the flesh is weak."....

And when He returned, He found them asleep again....

Then He came the third time and said to them, "Are you still sleeping and resting?" (Mark 14:33–41)

He swung the rod of reproof at the lazy church of Laodicea:

I know your works, that you are neither cold nor hot. I could wish you were cold or hot. So then, because you are luke-warm, and neither cold nor hot, I will vomit you out of My mouth. Because you say, "I am rich, have become wealthy, and have need of nothing"—and do not know that you are wretched, miserable, poor, blind, and naked.... As many as I love, I rebuke and chasten. Therefore be zealous and repent. (Rev. 3:15–19)

With the dazed pair on the road to Emmaus, Jesus resorts to affectionate admonition:

And He said to them, "What kind of conversation is this that you have with one another as you walk and are sad?"....

So they said to Him,... "Jesus of Nazareth, who was a Prophet mighty in deed and word before God and all the people...the chief priests and our rulers delivered...to be condemned to death, and crucified Him. But we were hop-ing that it was He who was going to redeem Israel. Indeed, besides all this, today is the third day since these things happened....

Then He said to them, "O foolish ones, and slow of heart to believe in all that the prophets have spoken!" (Luke 24:17–21, 25)

D. Martyn Lloyd-Jones comments on the significance of Jesus calling Cleopas and his sadness commiserating Emmaus road part-ner fools:

The tragedy is that we…are sentimental. Sentimentality is very largely the trouble with the present church. We are very nice people, we members of the Christian church, but we are very foolish. And the first thing we must do is wake up and think and understand the truth and begin to apply it to the situation in which we find ourselves, instead of giving way, instead of giving in, instead of just commiserating with one another. I am sometimes afraid that the church is dying of niceness. We are really good at praising one another, aren't we, and saying that we are doing well. We have become a mutual admiration society, sympathizing and communing with one another, and thus being sentimental with one another. And the whole time the condition of the church degenerates from bad to worse. *Fools!*[11]

So the healthy companion of adrenalized encouragement is spurring on to excellence, which often involves loving criticism. But be careful. This doesn't give us license to recklessly swing the machete of confrontational rebuke. This happens all too often, and Scripture has much to say about it:

There is one who speaks like the piercings of a sword,
But the tongue of the wise promotes health. (Prov. 12:18)

A true physician of souls carefully and delicately pares with a scalpel. It is a form of artistry:

A word fitly spoken is like apples of gold
In settings of silver.
Like an earring of gold and an ornament of fine gold
Is a wise rebuker to an obedient ear. (Prov. 25:11–12)

Writer Erik Larson captures the fine balance between praise and helpful criticism in his book *Dead Wake: The Last Crossing of the Lusitania*. In his acknowledgments, Larson thanks the various people who helped to make his book a success. But his words for

---

11. David Martyn Lloyd-Jones, *Setting Our Affections upon Glory: Nine Sermons on the Gospel and the Church* (Wheaton, Ill.: Crossway, 2013), 76.

his editor are telling: "My editor at Crown Publishing, Amanda Cook, wrote me an eleven page letter that provided a brilliant road map to tweaking the narrative. She proved a master at the art of offering praise, while at the same time shoving tiny knives under each of my fingernails, propelling me into a month of narrative renovation that was probably the most intense writing experience of my life."[12]

So if you are going to grab someone's face mask, it is best to combine it with messing up his hair because remember: giving encouragement is an adrenaline shot for someone's soul.

---

12. Erik Larson, *Dead Wake: The Last Crossing of the Lusitania* (New York: Crown Publishers, 2015), 339.

13

The Disposition of
ENCOURAGEMENT

And God saw that it was good.
—Genesis 1:10, 12, 18, 21, 25

"Find the Good." That is the saying on a plaque that hangs in our child's bedroom. It was handpicked by my wife, who knows this child as a kindred spirit. He tends to focus on the negatives and overlooks the positives. The motto is a prescription for godly living and thinking.

I've strived to convince you that we are all solemnly obligated to habitually breathe out encouragement by dispensing affirmation in its countless forms—commendation, boasting, approval, report, and recognition. If we are to do it, we need to "find the good." This requires us to travel through our days with our eyes wide open to the teeming good things that are out there. This "eyes-wide-open" mind-set imitates our heavenly Father, whom we are to image. He modeled it in the beginning.

God Finds the Good

At the beginning of this chapter, I quoted the refrain from Genesis 1, that God, as He looked on each part of His creation, "saw that it was good": the light, the dry land and the waters, the plants, the lights in the sky, sea creatures and birds, the animals—everything He made. Seven times in seven days, He saw it was good. Sam Crabtree has captured the profound truth here: "At the conclusion of each day of creation, God paused to comment on the goodness of it all. Affirmation is central to the universe, and it should be central in our lives as well, permeating all we do."[1]

You might be thinking, "Sure, but that was in prefall Paradise, before sin slithered in. Then sin cursed, polluted, and vandalized everything. Finding the good now, postfall, is surely obsolete—no longer a priority." But I think you're wrong. Maybe that is just your postfall default setting of "finding the bad" that plagues us, coming out of Eden. We can be negative and critical, having an eagle eye for the bad and a mole's eye for the good.

Ronald Reagan popularized the story of twin boys—one an extreme optimist and the other an extreme pessimist. A psychiatrist tried to treat each one. He put the pessimist into a room piled to the ceiling with brand-new toys, but he burst into tears, claiming that if he played with any of them, he would just break them. He then put the optimist into a room piled to the ceiling with horse manure, and he dug in gleefully with his bare hands, claiming there must be a pony in there somewhere! Edwin Meese, attorney general under Reagan, claimed that when things got tough in the Reagan White House, someone would inevitably shout, "There must be a pony in here somewhere!"[2]

Reagan's eye for finding the good was a godly trait that was biblically revealed in God's glorious character—even after the fall. God's eyes found good in Noah:

> Then the LORD saw that the wickedness of man was great in the earth, and that every intent of the thoughts of his heart was only evil continually. And the LORD was sorry that He had made man on the earth, and He was grieved in His heart. So the LORD said, "I will destroy man whom I have created from the face of the earth, both man and beast, creeping thing and birds of the air, for I am sorry that I have made

---

1. Crabtree, "How to Cultivate Encouragement in Your Church."
2. Tatiana Morales, "Writing for Ronald Reagan," *CBS News*, July 30, 2003, https://www.cbsnews.com/news/writing-for-ronald-reagan/.

them." But Noah found grace [favor NASB, ESV] in the eyes of the LORD.

This is the genealogy of Noah. Noah was a just [righteous, NASB, ESV] man, perfect in his generations. Noah walked with God. (Gen. 6:5–9)

Job was a man polluted with sin (Job 25:4), who poured out sin (38:2; 40:2), and needed to repent of sin (42:6). Yet the Lord found the good—much good—in Job to praise him for: "Then the LORD said to Satan, 'Have you considered My servant Job, that there is none like him on the earth, a blameless and upright man, one who fears God and shuns evil?'" (1:8).

Centuries later, the house of King Jeroboam of Israel became such a moral cesspool that his offspring were doomed to be eaten by either dogs of the field or birds of the air (1 Kings 14:11). But God found the good in one of his sons—Abijah: "And all Israel shall mourn for him and bury him, for he is the only one of Jeroboam who shall come to the grave, because in him there is found something good toward the LORD God of Israel in the house of Jeroboam" (1 Kings 14:13).

Some Christians wonder, "I know God loves me, but does He like me?" The truth is that God finds good things and good works in his born-again, Spirit-animated children that bring Him great delight and pleasure. Even though we are saved and regenerated, we are still plagued with the bad, but that doesn't keep our heavenly Father from finding the spiritual good. Romans 8:8–9 says, "Those who are in the flesh cannot please God. But you are not in the flesh but in the Spirit, if indeed the Spirit of God dwells in you."

So by implication, we who are born again, indwelled by the Spirit, can and do please God!

John Piper explains God's finding something to like in us:

> I know this is hard to believe and hard to feel for many people, because our experience is that, if there's any part of our lives that is imperfect, that's what others are going to pick up on and complain about. They're not going to spot anything

good and like us for it. They're going to spot what we haven't yet accomplished for goodness, and they're going to be displeased by it—and that's especially true of God, people feel. We can never really be liked, only tolerated, because the focus is always on our shortcomings rather than our little successes. I want to say loud and clear, God is not like that! Let me say it again, God is not like that! God sees the incremental advances of our transformation by his Spirit and delights in them.[3]

Jesus Finds the Good

Then consider our Lord Jesus—the One who was in the beginning God—became flesh and dwelled among us. He took up residence in our sin-cursed world. He daily walked with sinners—still with his eyes wide open, characteristically and graciously "finding the good." "Jesus saw Nathanael coming toward Him, and said of him, 'Behold, an Israelite indeed, in whom is no deceit!'" (John 1:47).

His ears were wide open too. In John 4, He requested of the woman at the well,

"Go, call your husband, and come here."
The woman answered and said, "I have no husband."
Jesus said to her, "You have well said, 'I have no husband,' for you have had five husbands, and the one whom you now have is not your husband; in that you spoke truly." (vv. 16–18)

As the Great Physician probes the sensitive area of her heart, she masks her guilt and hurt. But even in her evasive, half-truth maneuver, our Lord finds something good worth commending. Nineteenth-century clergyman and author J. C. Ryle comments, "This teaches us to make the best of a sinner's words.... An unskilled physician of souls would have probably rebuked the woman sharply for her wickednesss, but not our Lord."[4]

---

3. John Piper, "I Know God Loves Me, but Does He Like Me?," *Ask Pastor John*, Desiring God, June 12, 2017, https://www.desiringgod.org/interviews/i-know-god-loves-me-but-does-he-like-me.

4. J. C. Ryle, *Expository Thoughts on the Gospels: John*, commentary on John 4,

Nor is this atypical of Jesus. Consider how He encourages a variety of people:

> When Jesus heard it [from the Centurion], He marveled, and said to those who followed, "Assuredly, I say to you, I have not found such great faith, not even in Israel!" (Matt. 8:10)

> Assuredly, I say to you, among those born of women there has not risen one greater than John the Baptist; but he who is least in the kingdom of heaven is greater than he. (Matt. 11:11)

> Then Jesus answered and said to her, "O woman, great is your faith! Let it be to you as you desire." And her daughter was healed from that very hour. (Matt. 15:28)

> His lord said to him, "Well done, good and faithful servant; you have been faithful over a few things, I will make you ruler over many things. Enter into the joy of your lord." (Matt. 25:23)

> But when Jesus was aware of it, He said to them, "Why do you trouble the woman? For she has done a good work for Me." (Matt. 26:10)

> But one thing is needed, and Mary has chosen that good part, which will not be taken away from her. (Luke 10:42)

> For the hour is coming in which all who are in the graves will hear His voice and come forth—those who have done good, to the resurrection of life, and those who have done evil, to the resurrection of condemnation. (John 5:28–29)

In Revelation 2 and 3, the ascended Lord Jesus visits the seven churches of Asia Minor (Ephesus, Smyrna, Pergamos, Thyatira, Sardis, Philadelphia, and Laodicea). In each He finds something good and worthy of praise or commendation. The lone exception may be the vomit-you-out-of-My-mouth-worthy Laodicea, but even that church is encouragingly reassured of Christ's special affection: "As many as I love,… I…knock…I will come in…and dine" (3:19–20).

StudyLight.org, accessed May 30, 2018, https://www.studylight.org/commentaries/ryl/john-4.html.

Finally, Jesus takes our breath away by finding the good among His arguably disappointing and unworthy disciples in the upper room, as described in Luke 22:14–62. Jesus eagerly desired to eat that Passover with them before He suffered (v. 15). His omniscient eyes could see into the future, and He knew that in a few hours He would be spat on, blindfolded and struck in the head, stripped and scourged at a pillar, have spikes driven through His hands and feet, hang naked and suffocating, and endure hellish wrath in outer darkness. His all-knowing mind saw Himself soon agonizing to death in Gethsemane and staggering in anticipation.

So with subtlety He confided in His friends, divulging His coming suffering with the shadowy symbolism of the bread and the cup (Luke 22:17–21). He would selflessly sacrifice all for His friends! And how do these disciples respond? "Now there was also a dispute among them, as to which of them should be considered the greatest" (v. 24).

How disgusting and obscene! Seeking support and consolation in distress, Jesus instead gets egotism and self-absorption in return. Each disciple argued why he deserved the limelight and the popularity trophy. But troubled Jesus knew they would fall asleep in the garden, run away and abandon Him before the temple guard lanterns, and deny Him again and again in Caiaphas's courtyard.

In this upper room full of sinful human manure, I would have unleashed on their unworthy heads a scorching rebuke against their self-centered ingratitude! But not our Lord. Instead, after a tender caution, He finds the good and pours soothing oil on their heads through words of encouraging commendation: "But you are those who have continued with Me [stood by Me, NASB] in My trials. And I bestow upon you a kingdom, just as My Father bestowed one upon Me, that you may eat and drink at My table in My kingdom, and sit on thrones judging the twelve tribes of Israel" (Luke 22:28–30).

Jesus knew the upcoming gauntlet of temptation, opposition, and persecution His friends would have to run in order to remain faithful to Him. He knew that Peter would be sifted (Luke

22:31–34), that they all would be assaulted (vv. 35–37), and that they would together be hiding in terror in the upper room while He was lying dead in seeming defeat in the tomb.

Jesus knew that their ashamed and fainting souls would need the adrenaline of encouragement. Jesus knew that the memory of His words of reviving commendation would act as smelling salts to get them up off the mat so they could answer the bell after His resurrection. They would need to fight a good fight to the end! And they did.

In view of our Lord's relentless pattern of finding the good, we would do well to survey the wreckage of our frequently frustrating circumstances and supporting cast and ask the simple question, What would Jesus do? So, as our heavenly Father and our Lord Jesus habitually find the good and accordingly speak words of commending encouragement, we are solemnly obligated to imitate them by doing the same.

14

The Expansion of
ENCOURAGEMENT

I have yet to find the man, however exalted his station, who did not do better work and put forth a greater effort under a spirit of approval than under a spirit of criticism.
—Charles Schwab

A few weeks ago, our four-year-old grandson, Richard, spent the entire day at our house. We had done many things together— wrestled on the carpet, hit golf balls, chased each other around the house, and talked about how good he was at building Lego things. In the early evening, I dropped him and his two-year-old brother off at their home. They wanted to show me their "big" backyard. And they did. I left them in the backyard with their dad and returned to my car to head home. But while I was about to close the car door and drive away, Richard ran around the house to the front yard shouting, "Papa! Papa! Papa!"

"What?" I asked.

"Papa, I love you!" That little four-word affirmation from our grandson has become a canteen of sweet nectar encouragement that I've been sipping on for a few days now. It doesn't take much to brighten the eyes.

Let's conclude this book with a practical expansion on the many ways we can deliver godly shots of encouragement. Remember, encouragement is adrenaline. Consider four additional venues.

At School

Gordon Beld wrote a book creatively chronicling the history of my hometown, Grand Rapids, Michigan. In an introductory chapter, "Gratitude for Grand People," he expressed thanks for folks who significantly contributed to his impressive literary career:

> Martha Schuitema. As the principal and teacher of the seventh and eighth grades at the five-room Newhall School in suburban Wyoming Township, Mrs. Schuitema was a strict disciplinarian and nobody's favorite teacher. But she taught me all I know about grammar and mechanics so essential for my life's work.
>
> Kenneth Davis. Wyoming Park's principal, as well as my geometry and chemistry teacher, Mr. Davis knew that during my lackluster senior year of study, I was learning more at the *Grand Rapids Press* than in the classroom. So on mornings when I'd arrive at school hours late after spending time at the sports desk writing stories of the previous night's games, he'd always cheerfully sign a pass admitting me to class.[1]

Former students who thank their past teachers with just a Facebook note or message can give an eye-brightening shot to an aging and fainting heart. It gives teachers the satisfaction of knowing that they made a difference after all. I should really look up Mr. O'Malley, Mrs. Rens, and Mrs. VanHaitsma—my history, Latin, and English teachers.

Larry Crabb remembers being in a class when a young woman he didn't know offered an embarrassingly wrong answer during a lecture. She blushed, adjusted her skirt, and died a thousand deaths. Crabb's heart went out to her, and after class he intended to encourage her but felt inhibited and inclined to talk only with familiar classmates. Rationalizations to just forget it swarmed. But he pushed himself out of his comfort zone and over to her. He said, "I sensed that might have been a tough moment for you. It took a

---

1. Gordon Beld, *Grand Times in Grand Rapids: Pieces of Furniture City History* (Charleston, S.C.: History Press, 2012), 11–12.

lot of courage to answer the question the teacher asked. I respect that." The woman walked away…encouraged.[2]

Alex was a troubled junior high student who couldn't get any traction at his new school. But then Mr. Clemens volunteered to coach the middle school boys' basketball team. He saw Alex was struggling and took him under his wing and fed him a steady diet of praise and encouragement. With this relationship, Alex turned the corner and eventually blossomed.

Many of us recall parents, teachers, pastors, coaches, Sunday school teachers, and other special people who challenged us to do our best and seemed to bring out the best in us. Longtime professor at Dallas Theological Seminary Howard Hendricks recalled his sixth-grade teacher. He was a troubled boy from a broken home whose reputation preceded him. "Howard," she told him, "I've heard all about you. But I don't believe a word of it." Hendricks began to thrive under her loving direction and said later, "I would have walked through a wall for that woman."[3]

In the Marketplace

Every day we talk to people who could use a shot of encouragement. As discussed earlier, we know they're in need because they're breathing.

Dentists encounter a high rate of stress and disillusionment and are twice as likely to commit suicide as the general population. If yours is an outstanding craftsman like mine, tell him or her frequently how much you appreciate his or her excellent, ethical, and economical professionalism.

When you pass through that Illinois tollbooth just outside Chicago and you notice that your line of vehicles moves more swiftly than the other four lines and that it was due to a conscientious booth agent with swift hands, a polite voice, and a noble work

---

2. Crabb and Allender, *Encouragement*, 91–93.

3. As cited in "Hebrews 10:24–25 Commentary," Preceptaustin.org, accessed May 30, 2018, https://www.preceptaustin.org/hebrews_1024-25

ethic, tell him how much you appreciate his stand-out efforts. That kind of compliment can burst sunshine into an overcast booth.

When my barber, Frank, gives me a particularly well-crafted haircut (and of course, sometimes it takes a couple of days to recognize it), I've made it a point to pull into his parking lot, leave the car running, pop my head into his shop, and tell him he did a great job!

My son purchased a pullover for me for Christmas from his college bookstore, but it was too big. I called and talked to a worker at the store. She told me that they were out of my size, but she took down my name and said she would call me when they came in. It took over two months, but I got a voicemail from the young woman at the store telling me my size was available. Instead of just having my son exchange the pullover, I made a point to call her and tell her how impressed I was with her remembering.

We can do the same with phone bank workers, who can be treated unkindly all day by irritable people. An encouraging word expressing appreciation is priceless, and a single comment to a worker's manager for a job well done is precious, able to turn the tide of someone's career.

In Social Media

I know it is fashionable in some Christian circles to criticize and mock social media as a vast wasteland because so many users of it squander precious time and energy. Some Christians may even wear their ignorance and lack of knowledge about Facebook, Twitter, Instagram, and the blogosphere as a badge of spiritually minded honor. Surely John Piper, who uses Twitter extensively, has a valid point when he writes, "One of the great uses of Twitter and Facebook will be to prove on the Last Day that our prayerlessness was not from lack of time."[4]

---

4. As cited in Mark Dever, "12 Questions to Ask Yourself Before Posting Something Online," 9Marks, August 29, 2016, https://www.9marks.org/article/12-questions-to-ask-yourself-before-posting-something-online/.

But an attitude of aloof disregard toward cyberspace may be a shortsighted miscalculation. Did the apostle Paul boycott the Agora or Areopagus in Athens because they were the arenas for idle babblers to spout off about the latest-to-hatch nonsense in the empire? No, he went there and made his voice heard for the cause of truth:

> Now while Paul waited for them at Athens, his spirit was provoked within him when he saw that the city was given over to idols. Therefore he reasoned in the synagogue with the Jews and with the Gentile worshipers, and in the marketplace daily with those who happened to be there. Then certain Epicurean and Stoic philosophers encountered him. And some said, "What does this babbler want to say?"
>
> Others said, "He seems to be a proclaimer of foreign gods," because he preached to them Jesus and the resurrection.
>
> And they took him and brought him to the Areopagus, saying, "May we know what this new doctrine is of which you speak? For you are bringing some strange things to our ears. Therefore we want to know what these things mean." For all the Athenians and the foreigners who were there spent their time in nothing else but either to tell or to hear some new thing. (Acts 17:16–21)

Social media is the marketplace of ideas in our twenty-first-century global society. As Christians who are to be the light of the world, we can be useful there. Like diligent missionaries, we can learn the "foreign language" of web communication so we can connect with the culture of our generation. I don't mean just impacting faraway folks in distant countries and continents. I mean connecting with my local congregation, community, and extended family. We'll find them where they're at—conversing on social media.

Social media can be a rough-and-tumble place where hostile nastiness marks the language, and tenderhearted, encouraging kindness is all too infrequently expressed. We must conscientiously guard our communication on social media, realizing that it can be a destructive tool for belittling and harming, and make a point to use it as a constructive one for edifying and encouraging. Let's consider some adrenaline-shot examples.

Last year when my dear wife's birthday arrived and she was facing adding another digit to her age, a Facebook post appeared that parted the clouds. It was from our daughter, Abigail. It was accompanied by a gorgeous picture of my wife and Abbie just before Abbie's recent wedding with this emoticon-decorated caption: *"It's the Queen's Birthday Today!* I say 'queen' because she's the Queen of Kindness, the Queen of Hospitality, the Queen of Motherhood, the Queen of Giving, the Queen of Cooking. The Beauty Queen, and my Dad's Queen. Happy birthday, Mom!" Abbie's post was followed up with a comment by a friend named Peggy, who worked for years alongside my wife at a private school: "I agree! So glad I got to witness her also be the Queen of Education and Friendship!"

A young man who grew up in our church has gone on to bigger and better things as a nationally renowned athlete and a high-level military test flight engineer. But he still makes time to scroll through his newsfeed and frequently gives a thumb's up to many of my posts. I must admit that such friendly words of encouragement invigorate my heart.

Writer's block can suffocate the mind. I suffered from it a few months ago while writing this book. But then, out of cyberspace, came a post on my Facebook page: "Pastor Mark! Your book *Manly Dominion* has really helped me. It has literally changed my life. Thanks for writing it." These words of encouragement gave a blast of fresh air and filled my sails with wind for a couple of hours of inspired writing.

At the Workplace

The director/headmaster of the Christian school where my wife worked handed in his resignation as a result of physical and emotional burnout. He was so discouraged. When June rolled around, the staff held a farewell breakfast for their boss where he was showered with wonderful expressions of appreciation and encouragement. He was brought to tears, having just heard things he had never heard before. My wife came home from the breakfast shaking her head and commented, "It's so sad and unfortunate that he didn't constantly hear those very things as encouragements along the way."

A good leader nurtures his people. He cultivates lives by sowing words of encouragement. He lets things go to foster a culture of commendation. He takes time to write notes of appreciation. He stops in the middle of meetings and conversations to underscore good things people have done.

It has become popular for managers to help their employees improve by conducting a "360," where everyone in a person's circle is asked to point out his or her failings. Often the barrage of criticism is so overwhelming to the person that paralysis rather than improvement is the result. Martin Seligman recommends an alternative 360 that he calls "appreciative inquiry":

> Merciless criticism often makes us dig in our heels in defense, or worse, makes us helpless. We don't change. We do change however, when we discover what is best about ourselves and when we see specific ways to use our strengths more. I go into large organizations and get the whole workforce focused on what it is doing well. They detail the strengths of the corporation and tell stories about their coworkers at their very best.[5]

A man in our church worked for years at a regional bank's call center. His first manager was a Barnabas-like encourager, and he thrived under her strategy of finding the good in his telephone styles and strategies. He found himself typically near the top of the charts that evaluated performance and sales. Then that successful manager was promoted. Another manager, who drove his herd by criticism instead of leading with encouragement, was appointed. The effect on the man was devastating. He felt stressed, got nervous, lost sleep, lost his confidence, felt paralyzed, and experienced a sharp drop in his performance and sales numbers. Disheartened, he quit.

---

5. Martin E. P. Seligman, *Flourish: A Visionary New Understanding of Happiness and Well-Being* (New York: Free Press, 2011), 72.

In his book *Be Excellent at Anything,* Tony Schwartz presents a contrasting approach, citing research that displays how employees who felt they were fairly treated with care, had a 30-percent lower rate of coronary disease than those who felt they were not listened to and unfairly criticized.[6] American steel magnate Charles M. Schwab agreed: "I have yet to find the man, however exalted his station, who did not do better work and put forth a greater effort under a spirit of approval than under a spirit of criticism."

The date was October 31, 1942, during the dark days of World War II. Great Britain was having a tough time keeping men working in the coal mines. Most coal workers wanted to give up their dirty, thankless jobs to join the more glamorous military service. Winston Churchill was addressing a conference of coal-mine operators and miners in Westminster's Central Hall. Here is his speech finale:

> We shall not fail, and then some day, when children ask, "What did you do to win this inheritance for us, and to make our name so respected among men?" one will say: "I was a fighter pilot"; another will say: "I was in the Submarine Service"; another: "I marched with the Eighth Army"; a fourth will say: "None of you could have lived without the convoys and the Merchant Seamen"; and you in your turn will say, with equal pride and with equal right: "We cut the coal."[7]

Tears appeared in the eyes of hardened men, and they returned to their posts with steely resolve to dig the coal that powered the nation. And if that is the way it worked with fellow Englishmen digging for Great Britain, how much more should we use encouragement with fellow Christians fighting for Christ's kingdom? Giving encouragement provides shots of adrenaline for the soul. Let's get out there and do it.

---

6. Tony Schwartz, *Be Excellent at Anything: The Four Keys to Transforming the Way We Work and Live* (New York: Free Press, 2011), 129.

7. As cited in Joe McKeever, "Preacher, Get It Right!," Preaching.com, accessed May 30, 2018, https://www.preaching.com/articles/preacher-get-it-right/.

SCRIPTURE INDEX